Fr. ALESSIO PARENTE O.F.M. CAP.

"SEND ME YOUR GUARDIAN ANGEL"
PADRE PIO

Edited by
Fr. ALESSIO PARENTE O.F.M. CAP.

1st Edition

Our Lady of Grace Capuchin Friary
71013 San Giovanni Rotondo - FG - Italy
Phone: Friary (0882) 856109/Office 857584

Permission to publish is granted by Padre Pietro Tartaglia Provincial Minister, Capuchin.
Foggia, 9 November 1983.

SIGIL. FF. MIN. CAPPUCC. PROV. FODIAE

Visto: si permette la Stampa
P. Pietro Tartaglia
Ministro Provinciale Cappuccini
Foggia - 9 - Novembre - 1983

IN OBEDIENCE

In obedience to the Decree of Pope Urban VIII we declare that we do not attribute more than human faith to any extraordinary facts narrated in this book, nor do we anticipate the definitive judgement of the Church to which the editor intends to offer fullest submission.

WE WILL MEET AGAIN MY FRIEND

Bright laughing eyes,
to light my days,
Courage,
rare and true;
Kind words -
echoes of a loving heart,
I attribute to you.
But we will meet again,
my friend
on time's eternal shore,
We'll talk,
and laugh together then,
As we once did before.

Lorna H. Nevitt

V.Rev. Pietro Tartaglia R.I.P.

HE WALKS IN BEAUTY

HE WALKS IN BEAUTY
WHOSE HEART IS LIFTED UP
ABOVE THE THINGS OF EARTH
DEAF TO THE CLANG OF BELLS
AND THE SIREN'S SHRIEK.
WHO HEARS INSTEAD
THE RUSH OF ANGELS' WINGS
BEFORE THE THRONE OF GOD.

M. PARROTT

Some handicapped children from the Padre Pio S

ntre on the day of their first Holy Communion.

DESTINED TO THE CHAIR
CONSECRATED TO REST
TO THE WORLD
THEY HAVE ALREADY
GIVEN THEIR LIFE
THEIR TRIBUTE OF LIGHT
OF GOOD OF JOY

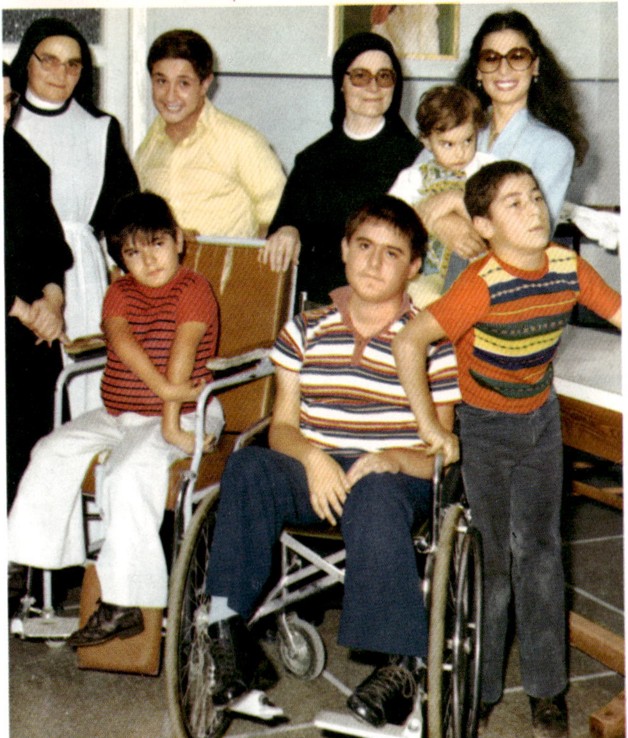

Any profit from this book will be used for Padre Pio's Spastic Centre.

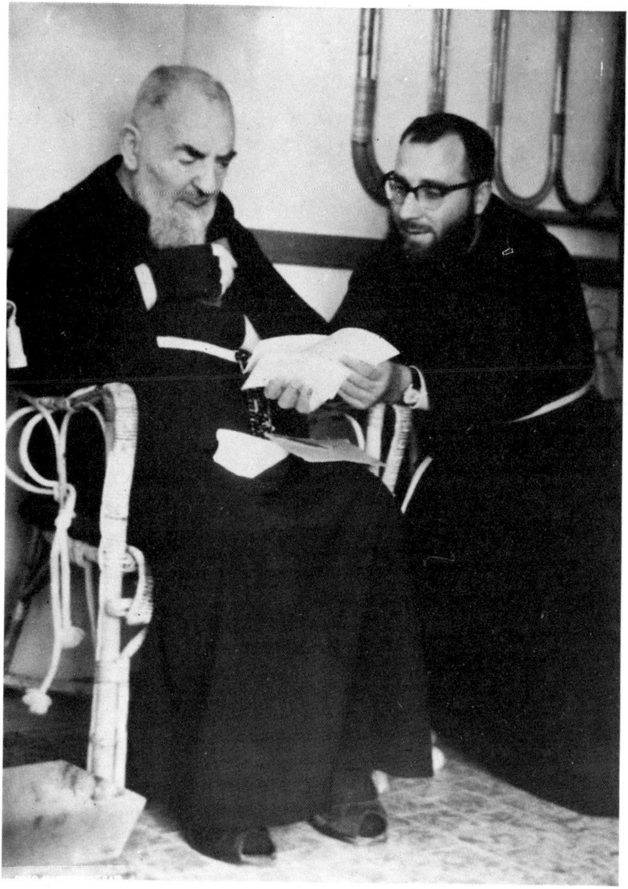

The author, Father Alessio, with our beloved Paure Pio.

I DEDICATE THIS BOOK TO ALL GUARDIAN ANGELS AND IN PARTICULAR TO MY OWN WHO HAS ACCOMPANIED AND PROTECTED ME THUS FAR THROUGH LIFE

To you
angel of goodness, heart of gold
my
sincere thanks
for
helping me to write this book.

For additional copies of this book write to:

Our Lady of Grace Capuchin Friary
71013 San Giovanni Rotondo (FG) Italy
Tel. Friary (0882) 856109 / Office 857584

or

at the tax deductible office:
National Centre for Padre Pio, Inc.
Vera M. Calandra, Director
11 N. Whitehall Rd.
Norristown, Pa. 19403 U.S.A
Tel. (215) 539 - 7779

or

The Irish Office for Padre Pio
Eileen Maguire, Director
8 Dufferin Avenue
S.C. Rd. Dublin 8. Ireland
Tel. (01) 753994

or

Padre Pio Centre of Australia
Capuchin Friars, Jersey Road
Plumpton 2761 N.S.W.
Australia

or

Philippine Centre for Padre Pio
JRC Ramrod Kartway Compound
E. Rodriguez Jr. Ave.
Libis, Quezon City, Metro Manila
Philippines

or

Padre Pio Information Centre
Stella M. Lilley
Kingsdown Park House
Whitstable, Kent CT5 2DF
England - Tel. (0227) 274050

CONTENTS

"For a good Angel will go with him; his journey will be successful and he will come back safe and sound."

Padre Pio and his ever-present companion Father Alessio are halted in their tracks by a "spiritual child" as they make their way through the Saint Francis room.

FOREWORD

"The best and most beautiful things in the world cannot be seen or even touched. They must be felt with the heart." *Helen Keller*

As an enthusiastic devotee of our beloved Padre Pio, I have read just about everything that exists, in the English language, concerning the great man. In my search for further reading material, I discovered that Father Alessio, who actually had the good fortune to live with Padre Pio, intended writing a book concerning Padre Pio and the Angels, so, needless to say, I was delighted.

In the past few years, the author of this book filled me in on his own personal experiences (which are many) with the Guardian Angels, and I was hooked! I mean, it is not every day that one reads of Angels laughing, Angels crying, Angels singing, Angels driving cars, mechanically-minded Angels, Angels of all trades, multilingual Angels.... is it? My total astonishment turned into an obsessive desire for further information as, day by day, I watched the book take shape.

The author, as I have already mentioned, spent a number of years at Padre Pio's side, so the information enclosed in this book comes "straight from the horse's mouth", so to speak. After a rather spasmodic beginning, due to his heavy work load, or perhaps the "evil interference", Father Alessio eventually got down to it and I believe that the reader will simply be amazed at the results. One, of course, could not be blamed for disbelieving many of the stories related within these pages, but they have not been plucked out of the air. On the contrary, the vast majority have been documented and testified to, or have been related to Father Alessio by people of sound character.

These angelic incidents have been

meticulously gathered together over a number of years and the author's humorous style of writing does not, by any means, conceal the serious matter therein. It would appear that he kept in mind the words of the famous Roman writer Horace, who said: "castigat ridendo mores" (through humour one can teach a sermon).

The object of this book is not to write anything new about the Angels, but to bring back the "old-fashioned" idea that we are all in the presence of a celestial companion who, as Padre Pio said: "does not abandon us, even when we disgust God". The Church Dogma on the Angels already tell us this, but in this book, we find out just how true it is, through the actual experiences of Padre Pio and his spiritual children with these very Angels.

One would hope, that through the reader's smiles, a definite message will come across, and that this message in turn, will bring the thoughts of many to their often forgotten companion, who, in complete silence, carries out his duty towards each one of us. If one were asked to sum up in a few words this little volume on Padre Pio and the Angels, one would have to say: To those who believe, it will increase their faith; to those who do not believe, they will at least begin to wonder.

Mary Bridget

INTRODUCTION

According to the revelations made to Mechtilde Schönwerth, who belonged to the Confraternity of Mary Queen of Hearts, and who, at her profession, took the name of Magdalen of the Cross, our knowledge of the Angels is a very limited one. From the Scriptures, Gospels and lives of the Saints, we know that myriads of Angels continuously serve men throughout the course of their earthly lives. Even though, in the Scriptures, these beings are mentioned 320 times, and at every main event in Christ's life, we still don't know too much about them; we don't honour them as they deserve.

In order to honour and love them we should first of all know them. If we would only understand their dignity, their perfection, their close relationship with God, their excellence and power, we would venerate them in an extraordinary way. Their love for us is immense and they guard our souls with great care because they witness God's great act of love for us. They know the high price paid by Christ for souls, so we should be inflamed with real love towards them and congratulate ourselves that we can greet them as our brothers and companions. We hardly know or think of our own Guardian Angel who is our constant companion throughout our whole life.

According to Magdalen of the Cross in her revelations, which were gathered together by Friederich von Lama, all Angels possess the same happiness. The knowledge of God is present to different degrees amongst the different Choirs, so that a higher Choir possesses a deeper knowledge of God. In this regard, Saint Michael and

Saint Gabriel excel all the other Angels. The Seraphim are completely inflamed with the fires of God's love and they possess perfect happiness. However, they can experience an accidental joy when they succeed in freeing a soul from the state of sin or prevent him from committing one. When they see that the merits of the Redemption are not lost, i.e. when a soul in their care reaches Heaven and praises God forever, they receive an accidental joy. The Guardian Angels exercise a continual watchfulness over souls committed to their care and once these souls reach Heaven to enjoy the vision of God, the Guardian Angel will remain there at their side.

The joy of the Guardian Angel is immeasurably increased when the souls entrusted to them enter Heaven, but in the case of lost souls, they are not deprived of their joy. God, in His infinite justice, increases their joy and assigns them to the special guard of the "Queen of Angels".

Guardian Angels differ from one another; some appear more active than others; some are more reserved, more timid. Those dressed in red and wearing a small crown are assigned to persons who suffer. Those dressed in white have always a joyful expression and wear a beautiful crown; they are assigned to innocent souls.

Children have especially beautiful Guardian Angels. Their garments are light-blue decorated with pearls, with a beautiful ever-lasting crown of roses around their heads. The Angels of sinners are dressed in garments of a deep red colour; they have their arms folded across their breasts and their faces turned towards Heaven in an imploring manner.

Holy souls who have a special mission on this earth have extraordinary Guardian Angels, who assist, defend and guide them throughout their lives. Amongst those souls was Padre Pio who had a very special one indeed. As a chosen soul who helped Jesus in His great work of Redemption, Padre Pio needed one with the attributes of all the Choirs; one who would have the kindness and meekness of The Angels, who would help him to bear the great bitterness which would come to him; count his sighs, dry his tears and strengthen him in his martyrdom; who would bring his prayers to the throne of God. He needed one who would have the strength and consolations of The Archangels, who would help him to be a warrior so that he could bear persecution for Christ's sake; who would be a messenger of God's commands and would have a special gift in the administration of the Sacrament of Penance. The power of The Virtues would help him to strive increasingly with all his soul to sanctify himself, through sacrifice and self-mortification, so that he might reach a high point of contemplative life. One who would have the compelling and authoritative character of The Powers, so that he could drive away all distraction during his obligatory prayers which would contribute towards his guidance of souls, especially loved by God.

The attributes of The Principalities would help him so that he could persevere in prayers and thus present, before the throne of God, all sacrifices, merits, prayers and good works of his spiritual children. He needed an Angel who would have the spiritual guidance of The Dominions, so that his teaching from the pulpit and his guidance from the confessional would increase the spreading of God's Kingdom on earth; convert heretics and bring back to God fallen-away catholics. One who would have the authority and majesty of The Thrones, so that in looking up to Heaven, he would present before the Blessed Trinity, with humility and fervour, all acts of mortification, prayers and good works of the seminarians in his care, augmented by his own merits, so that he could increase the faith and moral convictions of these young men on their way to the priesthood.

He needed one who would have the zeal of The Cherubim, so that he could stand ready at all times to defend the honour and glory of God and dissolve every doubt from those souls who approached him. The great love of The Seraphim would help him so that he could honour, praise and love the most Blessed Trinity, thus becoming a burning holocaust of love for the Fountain of Love.

Did Padre Pio have a Guardian Angel

with all these attributes? I would hasten to say that he did and as the following pages of this book unfold, I hope that it will become ever more evident to those who read. I place this book in the capable hands of my Guardian Angel, who, I feel sure, will be "at my side to light and guard, to rule and guide". I also send my Angel to Padre Pio to ask his help as he directed during his life time, when he said to all those souls who could not come personally to ask his prayers: "SEND ME YOUR GUARDIAN ANGEL".

Fr. Alessio Parente O.F.M. Cap.

WHO WAS PADRE PIO?

Padre Pio was born of simple hard-working farming people on 25 May 1887, in Pietrelcina, southern Italy. Already at the age of five he promised fidelity to Saint Francis of Assisi. On 6 January 1903, he entered the Capuchin Friary of Morcone, Benevento, where, on the 22nd. of that same month, he took the novices habit and the name Brother Pio. Of feeble health but strong will, with the help of grace he completed the required studies and was ordained a priest in 1910. He celebrated his first Mass in Pietrelcina where, except for a few interruptions, he remained until 1916.

In a letter from his home town dated 10 October 1915, he revealed to* Fr. Agostino that the Lord had already begun to favour him with celestial visions not long after his novitiate. He said that the Lord had given him the gift of the stigmata (invisible) in September 1910, and that for some years, almost once a week, he experienced the crowning with thorns and the flagellation.

On 17 February 1916, he left Pietrelcina completely and went to Foggia where he joined the community of St. Anne's Friary. Here he suffered terrible anguish caused by the work of the devil. On 28 July of the same year, he went, for the first time, to San Giovanni Rotondo, where, except for brief periods, he would remain for the rest of his life.

The year 1918 was a year filled with heavenly gifts for him as he received, for the first time, the visible signs of Christ's crucifixion on his body. The years 1919 - 33

* - Agostino da San Marco in Lamis his Spiritual Director.

were difficult and painful ones for Padre Pio: doctors visits, repeated intervention by the Holy Office; doubts as to whether he would be able to remain in San Giovanni Rotondo, accusations of various kinds etc. This culminated in the last two years (1931 - 33) with many deprivations; he could no longer hear confessions nor was he allowed to say Mass in public. He could only celebrate in the Friary's private chapel.

On 16 July 1933, Padre Pio once again took up his priestly ministry celebrating Mass in the public church. And in the following years the influx of people coming to San Giovanni Rotondo constantly increased, especially after World War II. Countless numbers were attracted to his confessional and many more received his saintly counsel and spiritual guidance through correspondence. His whole life was marked by long hours of prayer and continual austerity. His letters to his Spiritual Directors reveal his ineffable sufferings, physical and spiritual, which accompanied him all through life. They also reveal his very deep union with God, his burning love for the Blessed Eucharist and Our Lady.

Worn out by over half a century of intense suffering and constant apostolic activity in San Giovanni Rotondo, he was called to his heavenly reward on 23 September 1968. After a public funeral which attracted almost 100,000 people, his body was entombed in the crypt of Our Lady of Grace Church. Increasing numbers flock to his tomb from all parts of the world and many testify to spiritual and temporal favours received. On 16 February 1973, the Archbishop of Manfredonia, Mgr. Valentino Vailati, consigned the documentation to the Congregation for the Causes of Saints so as to obtain the "nihil obstat" for the beginning of the Process for his beatification. Further documents were presented to the Holy Congregation on 3 March 1980 and on 29 November 1982, His Holiness, Pope John Paul II approved the decree for the opening of the Canonical Informative Process on the life and virtues of the Servant of God, Padre Pio of Pietrelcina. The official opening of the

Canonical Informative Process took place on 20 March 1983.

Significant Dates:

Birth	-	25	May	1887
Baptism	-	26	May	1887
Confirmation	-	27	Sept.	1899
Taking of the Habit	-	22	Jan.	1903
Temporary Stigmata	-	?	Sept.	1910
Transverberation	-	5-7	Aug.	1918
Visible Stigmata	-	20	Sept.	1918
Death	-	23	Sept.	1968
Opening of preliminary Process	-	4	Nov.	1968

Presentation of the documents to the Holy Congregation for the Causes of Saints	-	16	Feb.	1973
Pope John Paul II approves the decree for the opening of the Canonical Informative Process on the life and virtues of the Servant of God Padre Pio of Pietrelcina	-	29	Nov.	1982
Official opening of the Canonical Informative Process	-	20	March	1983

"COMPANION OF MY INFANCY"

"For a good angel will go with him; his journey will be successful, and he will come back safe and sound." (Tob 5:21)

Father Eusebio, who assisted Padre Pio from 1961 to 1965, writing on the Guardian Angels and Padre Pio, said: "He began his work early when Padre Pio was still a boy. He took the semblance of another child and made himself visible to him. Later on, advanced in age and sanctity, Padre Pio will rightly call his Guardian Angel 'the companion of my infancy'. This name reveals an intimate relationship between the little Francesco and his dear Angel. A companion is not a person whom we see once or rarely, but a person whom we often see and with whom we are friends. We love him and, in the case of the child Padre Pio, play games too.... He had a heavenly friend who gladdened his boyhood and made him long for Heaven."

Meditating on the above facts reported by Padre Eusebio, we discover a reality so usual to Padre Pio but unknown to us. A reality much more impressive when we think that Padre Pio was a man so close to us and full of humanity; a man who lived and acted like any other human being but who also touched the highest spheres of the supernatural world; the world where he nourished his spirit. It is this "companion of my infancy" who will also be the companion of his whole life.

Fr. Eusebio continues: "This Angel will be near him when he leaves the world to devote himself to God; he will help him in the year of his novitiate, during his studies and preparation for the priesthood, and will take care that Padre Pio will be a worthy minister of Christ. He will lead him along the path of extraordinary sanctity and will be near him when he will have to experience the assaults of the devil, who seems to leave Hell and forget the rest of the world to fight the young friar. The Angel will never abandon Padre Pio in his struggle which will explode at Venafro* but which will last all his life.

"That's why Padre Pio had for his Angel a deep felt, most tender and confidential devotion which cancels out any differences between them and makes Padre Pio an Angel or makes his Guardian Angel a human creature. This connection will grow constantly as the years go by and as the Padre moves closer towards that sanctity to which God has called him."

---

* - More information on which can be found in the following chapter.

"AN ANGEL LAUGHS!"

"... *Let us worship and bow down...*"
(Ps 95:6)

During the month of October, 1911, Padre Pio, who at that time was a priest for little more than a year, came from Pietrelcina to Venafro (a small town in the Province of Isernia). Here, together with other young priests, he was under the guidance of Father Agostino of San Marco in Lamis. He became very ill and was sent to Naples to have a medical check but the doctors understood little or nothing. When he returned to Venafro, he could not celebrate Mass because of his illness, therefore he received Holy Communion, which was his only sustenance for 21 days.

After a while, his ecstasies were discovered, during which he remained in lengthy conversation with Jesus, Mary, his Guardian Angel and sometimes Saint Francis. The devil, whom he sometimes called "birbaccione" (scoundrel) was already in the back-ground and indeed his ecstasies were always either preceeded or followed by a diabolical apparition.

Padre Agostino, to the best of his ability, transcribed the words spoken by Padre Pio in some of his ecstasies. These were notes written in pencil, which he took feverishly while in the same room as Padre Pio, who begged his company. In these ecstasies, Padre Pio's Guardian Angel played a prominent role; spoke to him and laughed at him while Padre Pio playfully teased him. The following is an excerpt from one of his ecstasies and is dated by Fr. Agostino 29 November 1911:

"... Angel of God, my Angel... are you not taking care of me?... Are you a creature of God?... Either you're a creature of God or a creator... You're a creator? No. Therefore

you are God's creature and you have laws which you must obey... You must stay beside me whether you want to or not... He laughs... what is there to laugh about? Tell me one thing... you must tell me... who was here yesterday morning?... and he laughs... you must tell me... who was it?... Either Father Agostino or the Superior... tell me then... was it perhaps their secretaries? Answer me now... If you don't answer me I will say it was one of those four... He laughs... an Angel laughs!... Tell me then... I won't leave you until you tell me...

"If not, I will ask Jesus... and then you'll catch it!... Anyway, I won't ask that little Mother, that Lady... who looks at me so grimly... She's there in a bad humour... Jesus, isn't it true that your Mother is in a bad humour?... She laughs!...

"Now then, little man (his Guardian Angel), tell me who it was... No answer... he's there... like a fixture... I want to know... one thing I asked you and I'm here a long time... Jesus, you tell me... (It is assumed that there his Angel answers).

"It took a lot for you to say it, little

man!... you made me chatter on a lot!... yes, yes, Father Agostino... very well, my Angel, will you save him from the war prepared by the evil one? You will save him... Jesus, tell me, why do you permit it?... You don't want to tell me?... You will tell me... If you don't appear any more, very well... but if you do, I will have to tire you... And that little Mother... always with the corner of Her eye... I want to look you in the face... You must look straight at me... She laughs... and She turns Her back to me... yes, yes, laugh... I know that you love me... but you must look at me clearly.

"Jesus, why don't you tell your Mother?... but tell me, are you Jesus?... say, 'Jesus!'... Very well, if you are Jesus why does your Mother look at me in that manner?... I want to know!...

"Jesus, when you come again, I want to ask you certain things... You know what... but for now, I want to mention them to you... what were those flames in my heart this morning?... If it was not Rogerio (Fr. Rogerio who was with Padre Pio at that time) who embraced me tightly... and then

Fr. Agostino... my heart wanted to flee... what was it?... perhaps it wanted to go for a walk?... another thing... that thirst?... My God... what was it? Last night, when the Superior and Father Agostino left me, I drank a whole bottle, (of water) but it did not quench my thirst... It devoured me... and it tortured me until Communion... What was it? Listen, little Mother, it doesn't matter that you look at me like that... I love you more than all the creatures on earth and in Heaven... after Jesus, of course, but I love you.

"Jesus, will the evil one come tonight?... Well, help those two who assist me, protect and defend them... I know, you are there... but... Angel of mine, stay with me! Jesus, one last thing... let me kiss you... Fine!... how sweet are these wounds!... they bleed... but this blood is sweet... is sweet... Jesus, sweetness... Holy Host... Love, Love that sustains me, Love... until we meet again! (a rivederci)..."

I think that most of us would be amazed at the apparent intimacy between

Padre Pio, the Madonna, Jesus and his Guardian Angel. The broken sentences from the afore-mentioned ecstasy portray a picture of a little family group, chatting and teasing one another; scolding when necessary and telling of their affection at the opportune moment. The deep love between Padre Pio and his heavenly Visitors is totally evident. Padre Pio is completely at home; no awkwardness or embarrassment can be found and his camaraderic with his Guardian Angel is without doubt.

Eavesdropping on another ecstasy of December 1911, Padre Agostino transcribed the following:

"My Jesus, why do you seem so very young this morning? You have become so small. My Guardian Angel, do you see Jesus? Well then, bow to him!... That is not enough... Kiss his wounds... Fine... Good!... Angel of mine... Well done little child... Now, now he becomes serious... he pouts... what am I to call you?... What is your name?... But you understand, Angel of

mine, forgive me, you understand... Bless Jesus for me..."

During another ecstasy dated by Father Agostino 3 December 1911, whilst in conversation with Jesus and Our Lady, Padre Pio breaks off suddenly saying:

"... Ah, who calls me?... Angel of mine, let me stay with Jesus... Oh my Jesus, my sweetness, my love, love that sustains me... until we meet again!... But where?... In Paradise?... But tell me, my Jesus, where am I?... On earth... Ah, and what will be up there?... But my Jesus, tell me one thing: when the Father Superior calls me, who knocks at my door?... Ah, it's you my little Angel?... It's you, little boy?... Look... he becomes serious!... I call you Angel and you don't come immediately to help me, I have to beg you... I call you little boy... and you become serious... what a way to behave! You understand, Angel of mine, forgive me, you understand... Bless Jesus also for me..."

What can one say? Each time I read this beautiful passage I am at a loss for words, and that is not good for me if I wish to continue writing this book! Something which stands out, to my mind, is the fact that every time Padre Pio refers to his Guardian Angel as a "little boy", the "little man" becomes cross! Surely there is a lesson to be learned here. So, my dear readers, every time you talk to your Guardian Angel, be careful what you call him!

THE MULTILINGUAL ANGEL

"... (They) began to speak in other tongues, as the Spirit gave them utterance." (Acts 2:4)

In early 1912 an original idea occurred to Father Agostino of San Marco in Lamis, Padre Pio's confessor. To test Padre Pio's sanctity and to attack the devil, he decided to write in languages which Padre Pio did not know. So, a correspondence in Greek and French began between the Padre and his confessor. Padre Pio brilliantly overcame the trial; he had somebody translate the letters for him. Do you think it was a cleverer friend of his, or a more learned person? Well, one could say that, as it was in fact, his Guardian Angel!

There is authentic proof of this. When

Padre Pio received this strange correspondence, he was at Pietrelcina for medical reasons and was under the direct care of the local parish priest, Don Salvatore Pannullo. At the end of one of these letters (Letters I, No. 97), there is an autographed testimony by the above mentioned priest who, under oath, testified that Padre Pio, having received the letter written in Greek by his confessor, explained its exact contents to himself:

Pietrelcina, 25 August 1919.
"I, the undersigned, testify under oath, that when Padre Pio received this letter, he explained its contents to me literally. When I asked him how he could read and explain it, as he did not know even the Greek alphabet, he replied: 'You know, my Guardian Angel explained it all to me.' "
Signed
The parish priest Salvatore Pannullo

Besides this testimony, we have personal confirmation from Padre Pio

"Angel of God, my Angel... are you not taking care of me?"

Padre Pio

"With the help of my good Guardian Angel that wretch has been vanquished this time in his wicked design and your letter has been read."

Padre Pio

"Don't worry, the Angel of the Lord will go with you."
Padre Pio

"Don't worry. There is someone (Fr. Alessio) who takes good care of me."

Padre Pio

himself. When Father Agostino asked him how he got to know foreign languages, he answered with Jeremiah's words: "Ah, nescio loqui" (Letters I Nos. 75,76) that is: * "Ah, Lord God, I do not know how to speak."

In a letter dated 20 September 1912 (Letters I No. 98), Padre Pio reveals who his teacher is. He says: "The heavenly beings continue to visit me and to give me a foretaste of the rapture of the blessed. And while the mission of our Guardian Angels is a great one, my own Angel's mission is certainly greater, since he has the additional task of teaching me other languages."

This statement of Padre Pio is confirmed by Father Agostino who, in his * "Diario" (Diary) says: "Padre Pio does not understand either Greek or French; his

---

* - (Jer 1:6).

* - In Italian only.

Guardian Angel explained everything to him and he replied to me in like manner."

The help of this extraordinary teacher is so effective that Padre Pio was even able to write in foreign languages. In fact, amongst his letters recently published in English, are some, parts of which he wrote in French, from his Guardian Angel's dictation (e.g. Letters I Nos. 76, 82, 95, 96).

We have discovered that our beloved Padre found no difficulty in understanding the French and Greek languages due to his special heavenly aid. Later on in his life, it would appear that he even overcame the barrier of the English language, perhaps, also, with the help of his little "companion". Let me explain:

The story was told by Angelina Serritelli. Her brother, Tommasino, was living in America and, when his daughter reached the age when she should receive her first Holy Communion, he brought her to San Giovanni Rotondo to receive from the hands of Padre Pio. The little girl didn't know any Italian at all, so she was confided to Mary Pyle's care (of whom more will be read in a later chapter). On the day before the little girl should receive Jesus for the first time, Mary Pyle, who knew the usual procedure in these cases, brought her to Padre Pio: "Padre Pio", she said, "I brought this little girl to you so that she could confess to you." And Padre Pio: "Fine!" Mary continued: "Father, I'm here to help you as the little girl doesn't understand any Italian at all." "Mary", said Padre Pio, "you can go, as the little one and I will take care of this." After the confession, Mary, who was waiting for the girl, asked her: "Did Padre Pio understand you?" "Yes", came the reply. "And you understood him?" The same answer: "Yes". Mary, a little surprised, asked one more question: "Did he speak in English?" "Yes, in English", said the little girl.

Just as in the cases of the letters written in French and Greek, Padre Pio did not understand English, so how did he speak the language? Perhaps it was his Guardian Angel on the job once again.

I believe that in each one of these little experiences of Padre Pio with his Guardian

Angel, there is a lesson for each one of us. What is the lesson in this case? Perhaps here it is particularly directed to students of foreign languages. If you wish to improve your command of the language of another country, ask your Guardian Angel's help.

EVIL INTERFERENCE

"Now war broke out in Heaven, when Michael with his Angels attacked the dragon. The dragon fought back with his angels but they were defeated and driven out of Heaven."
(Rv 12:7-8)

Padre Pio's correspondence with his Spiritual Directors was often interfered with by the devil Padre Eusebio tells us: "Always with regard to the correspondence the devil was up to all sorts of mischief, but Padre Pio's Angel reveals satan's plans and the way to overcome them." One day, Padre Pio received a letter which was unreadable because of a large ink-blot over it. Satan wanted to prevent Padre Pio from reading it but his Guardian Angel came to his help. It is Padre Pio himself who tells us: "With the help of my good Guardian Angel that wretch has been vanquished this time in his wicked design and your letter has been read. The Angel had suggested to me to sprinkle your letters with holy water before opening them. I did this with your last but cannot tell you how enraged the ogre was. He wants to put an end to me at all costs and is using all his diabolical cunning to this end; but he will be crushed. The Angel assures me of this and Paradise is with us." (Letters I No. 108)

Saints of all ages have found strength and courage in David's familiar words: "The Angel of the Lord encamps around those who fear Him, and rescues them." (Ps 34:7) The Angel of the Lord delivered Daniel from the fangs and claws of the lions and Padre Pio was helped in his combats with satan, many times, by his Angel.

If he progressed along the path of sanctity, besides the help from Heaven, the merit for this also belongs to his confessor and Spiritual Director, to whom he manifested all the secrets of his soul. But this displeased the devil who tried, by various means to prevent it. In fact, one day satan took the semblance of a friar and went to Padre Pio telling him that, by order of the Provincial, he mustn't write to his confessor anymore: "... as it is against poverty and a serious obstacle to perfection... I should never have even faintly suspected this to be one of the ogre's snares", writes Padre Pio, "if the Angel had not revealed the fraud to me. Only Jesus knows how hard it was to convince me. The companion of my childhood tries to lessen the pains which those impure apostates inflict on me, by cradling my soul in a dream of hope." (Letters I No. 108)

Further confirmation of the devil's desire to cut any communication of his with his Spiritual Director can be found in letter No. 115, when Padre Pio, writing to Father Agostino, says: "... When I received your letter recently, and before I had opened it, those wretches told me to tear it up or else throw it in the fire. If I did this, they would withdraw for good and would not trouble me again. I kept silent without giving them any answer while in my heart I despised them. Then they added: 'We want this merely as a condition for our withdrawal. In doing so you will not be showing contempt for anyone.' I replied that nothing would make me change my mind and they flung themselves on me like so many hungry tigers." (Letters I No. 115)

In the lives of the Saints we find similar occurrences to those experienced by Padre Pio, noticably so in the life of Magdalen of the Cross, so let us take a few examples. She wrote: "My Archangel warned me to be on my guard whenever an Archangel appeared to me. I should observe closely whether there was a cross on his stole and if not, I must command him in the name of Jesus to say who he is. I shall remember this."

Having received this advice, she certainly took it into account and later wrote: "I was bothered today quite a bit by a beautiful Angel who did not have a cross on his stole. He repeatedly told me that, since I was destined to be damned anyway, I should make my life as comfortable as possible and that he would help me. If I had no particular desire for earthly happiness, I should simply end my life because it was wholly worthless. This second temptation was so violent that I called my Archangel to help me and the fallen angel disappeared."

The devil appeared to Padre Pio in many forms including that of his Guardian Angel but he always discovered the deception by pronouncing the words: "Long live Jesus!" and with that, the evil spirit disappeared.

At this point, I must mention a personal experience of mine concerning Padre Pio and the evil interference. Although it does not directly concern the Guardian Angels, I think it is very worthwhile relating as it shows just how much he was persecuted by the devil:

One night, during the time when I was looking after him, I washed his face, combed his hair, undressed him and helped him into bed. Having done this, and seeing that he was in need of nothing, I slipped away to my room. I had only reached it, when the bell, with which he used to summon me, rang. I rushed back to his cell, and when I approached him, he didn't say a word; he simply smiled at me. Now, I'm always happy to receive a smile from our beloved Padre, but on this occasion I was feeling more tired than usual so, I'm ashamed to say, I was a little put out.

I went back to my room and the bell rang again. Once more, I went to see what was wrong, but he said nothing and just bestowed on me another radiant smile. This happened at least ten times until eventually, I said: "Father, you call me here, but when I arrive, instead of telling me what you want, you just smile at me. If you don't let me sleep, it will be you who will have to assist me tomorrow, and not me you!" I will never forget the manner in which he looked at me on that occasion. His eyes were filled with profound suffering as he said to me: "Please, my son, will you sleep on the chair here beside me, because the devils won't leave me for one minute tonight."

I understood immediately what he meant, so I settled myself on the arm-chair in his room and there I dozed. Now and then, I would look to see how he was, and I could distinctly hear him whispering the Hail Mary. He seemed no longer afraid, as perhaps my presence there prevented the devil from beating him and throwing him out of bed. I, with a marked lack of humility, like to think, that that night, I functioned as Padre Pio's Guardian Angel.

However, throughout all these attacks of the devil, he was constantly in the presence of his good Angel who always came to his aid whenever the need arose. Well, almost whenever the need arose... There were some occasions when his friend was not so quick on the job, and on these occasions Padre Pio gave him the sharp end of his tongue as the reader will discover in the following story...

A GOOD SCOLDING

"Angels of the Lord, all bless the Lord.
Give glory and eternal praise to Him."
(Dn 3:58)

Padre Pio's Guardian Angel, although undoubtedly a member of the fast messenger corps of Heaven, sometimes was not so fast when Padre Pio himself was in need of his presence. In fact, he wrote to Father Agostino: "... I cannot tell you the way these scoundrels beat me. Sometimes I feel that I am about to die. On Saturday it seemed to me that they intended to put an end to me and I did not know which Saint to invoke. I turned to my Guardian Angel and, after he had kept me waiting a while, there he was, hovering close to me, singing hymns to the Divine Majesty in his angelic voice." (Letters I No. 102)

The scolding and the row, if the reader will pardon the expression, was inevitable. You can imagine, Padre Pio on the floor severely beaten by the devils; beaten black and blue, while his "friend" and "companion", instead of immediately coming on the scene, keeps him waiting. Then, to add insult to injury, when he does appear, instead of chasing the devils away he starts to sing hymns!!! The scene is almost impossible to imagine: a severe attack by the devils; an imploring, helpless Padre Pio; a careless friend (his Guardian Angel); the much implored help appears but instead of helping, he sings loudly with joy!

Then the scolding and the row which were inevitable. The punishment was obligatory: "... I rebuked him bitterly for having kept me waiting for so long when I had not failed to call him to my assistance. To punish him, I did not want to look him in the face; I wanted to get away; to escape from him. But he, poor creature, caught up with me almost in tears and held me until I raised my eyes to his face and found him all upset." (Letters I No. 102)

His little friend, in tears, begs Padre Pio's forgiveness. The friendship is re-established with the words of the Guardian Angel: "... I am always close to you, my beloved young man", he said. "I am always hovering around you with the affection aroused by your gratitude to the Beloved of your heart. This affection of mine will never end, not even when you die. I know that your generous heart beats all the time for the One we both love. You would cross every mountain and every desert in search of Him; to see Him again; to embrace Him again in these extreme moments and to ask Him at once to break this chain which unites you to the body... that far from Him you may no longer suffer so much; that He take you to Himself. Tell Him that separated from Him you reap more sorrow than joy. This is precisely the gift you want from Him; but do not grow weary, you must wait a little longer. For the present He can give you nothing like the ray of a star, the perfume of a flower, the caress of the wind! But do not cease to ask Him insistently for this, because His supreme delight is to have you with Him. And although He cannot satisfy you, as Providence wills that you remain in exile a little longer, He will gratify you in the end, at least in part..." (Letters I No. 102)

With this beautiful little speech from his Guardian Angel, Padre Pio could scold no longer. Writing to Father Agostino he said: "Poor little Angel! He is too good. Will he succeed in making me understand the serious duty of gratitude?"

What a beautiful lesson on patience from Padre Pio's Guardian Angel. What a lesson to us who sometimes want things done our own way; who want to obtain things that please us, but, as Padre Pio's companion said, we must remain "in exile a little longer" even though Jesus delights in having us with Him. And as regards the lesson on gratitude; I think most of us are inclined to take everything for granted. We believe, generally speaking, that we should reach Jesus in the easiest manner possible, forgetting that we are in exile and that

Heaven can be reached only if we suffer without "any consolation"; if we become victims; if we understand the full meaning of "consummatum est" (it is finished) and "in manus tuas" (into your hands). "My son", said Jesus to Padre Pio, "love is recognized through suffering; you will feel it acutely in your soul and even more acutely in your body."

In his soul, suffering came to him through the continuous trials of the devil; in his body, from the physical suffering which oppressed him throughout the entire span of his life. Sometimes, Padre Pio, like any other human being, complained about his sufferings as can be seen from the following letter which he wrote to Father Agostino: "I complained to my Guardian Angel", he said, "and after giving me a little sermon, he continued: 'Thank Jesus who is treating you as one chosen to follow him closely up the steep ascent of Calvary; soul confided by Jesus to my care, I behold with joy and deep emotion this behaviour of Jesus towards you. Do you perhaps think I would be so happy if I did not see you ill-treated like this? I, who in holy charity greatly desire your good, rejoice more and more to see you in this state. Defend yourself, always reject and despise the devil's evil insinuations, and when your own strength is not sufficient, do not be distressed, beloved of my heart, for I am close to you' " (Letters I No. 113)

Did we ever experience such love and affection from our Guardian Angel? If not, perhaps it is because we do not have so much trust and confidence in him as Padre Pio did in his. Perhaps if we were to search deep down in ourselves, we would discover that we doubted, to some small degree, the ability of this, our Angel, or even his very existence. "The cleverest trick of the devil is to convince us that he doesn't exist", said Carlo Baudelaire. Perhaps, too, it is his work that makes us sometimes doubt or forget this "companion" by our side.

PUNCTUAL ANGEL

"... Get up!... hurry!" (Acts 12:7-11)

It seems that the Angels are well practised in the art of waking people up from their peaceful slumber. Throughout the Bible we come across incidents when they did just that. When Saint Peter was in prison, the Angel of the Lord came to him and told him to get up: "Suddenly the Angel of the Lord stood there and the cell was filled with light. He tapped Peter on the side and woke him. 'Get up', he said, 'hurry!', and the chains fell from his hands. The Angel then said: 'Put on your belt and sandals.' After he had done this, the Angel next said: 'Wrap your cloak round you and follow me.' Peter followed him but had no idea that what the Angel did was happening in reality; he thought he was seeing a vision. They passed through two guard posts, one after another, and reached the iron gate leading to the city. This opened of its own accord; they passed through it and had walked the whole length of one street when suddenly the Angel left him. It was only then that Peter came to himself. 'Now I know it is all true', he said. 'The Lord really did send his Angel and has saved me from Herod and from all the Jewish people were so certain would happen to me' " (Acts 2:7-11)

And also when the Christ Child was on earth: "After Herod's death, the Angel of the Lord appeared in a dream to Joseph in Egypt and said: 'Get up, take the Child and his Mother with you and go back to the land of Israel, for those who wanted to kill the Child are dead.' " (Mt 2:19-20)

When I was assisting Padre Pio from 1959 to 1961, and from 1965 to 1968, because of the attacks of the devils, the comings and goings of the Guardian Angels and his continuous ill-health, I was constantly called to his side; so much so, that I did not have enough time for sleep. Perhaps the reader will be amused to hear that the only time for me to get some sleep was when Padre Pio was saying Mass and during the time when he was hearing confessions. When he was about to say Mass, I would customarily remove the woolen mittens from his hands, accompany him to the altar and, having completed this, I would run straight to my room, throw myself on the bed and within a few minutes, fall sound asleep, like a log!

It was my duty to assist Padre Pio from the altar at the end of Mass, as I had to guide him through the sacristy to the solitude of his cell. Many times my alarm clock did not wake me up as I was so deeply asleep, or sometimes, half asleep, half awake, I would switch it off. Everytime I overslept, I heard a knocking at my door, so realizing I was late, I would jump out of bed and run out into the long corridor to see who called me, but there was nobody there. I would race down to the church and there I invariably found Padre Pio, at the end of the Mass giving the last blessing.

The same thing happened when he went to hear confessions: I accompanied him to the confessional box, helped him to sit down, then ran to my room, set the alarm clock and went straight to sleep. However, as usual, my alarm clock served no purpose. Nevertheless, I always heard a voice in my deep sleep saying: "Alessio, Alessio, come down!" Realizing I was late, I would run down to the little church and there I always found Padre Pio waiting for me. Usually, he would not leave the confessional unless there was someone at his side. Not only was he not able to walk alone through the crowds, but he knew that if he so much as attempted it, he would reach his room with his habit in pieces. Italian women were well equipped with scissors and they would not be shy about using them to cut a relic for themselves.

The conclusion to this little story is as follows: One day I was sitting by Padre

Pio's side in the sitting-room, adjacent to his cell and that had been one of those days during which I had not heard the alarm, both for the end of Mass and the end of his time in the confessional box. I was feeling very much ashamed at my lack of punctuality and I was trying to explain to Padre Pio that I had not heard the alarm, but he interrupted me saying: "Yes, I understand you. But do you think I will continue to send my Guardian Angel every day to wake you up? You'd better go and buy yourself a new alarm clock."

It was only then that I realized who was knocking at my door and calling me in my sleep. It was Padre Pio's Guardian Angel!

Well, yes, I was rather remiss on occasion whilst looking after Padre Pio, but maybe not quite so careless as the reader would think. In fact, I am told that Padre Pio appreciated very much the devoted manner in which I took care of him as we will see from the following letter which he wrote to Cleonice Morcaldi, who was a close friend of his. He said: "My little daughter, don't let your imagination work too much; this imagination of yours which is urged on by the heart. Don't worry, there is somebody who takes care of me. Father Alessio is good-hearted, and is like a little faithful puppy-dog. I greet you in Jesus and Mary." Padre Pio

What a joy to have ones-self referred to in this manner by our beloved Padre. The above quoted letter is one I will treasure for the rest of my days and often, when I find the going tough here, workwise, I pick it up and it never fails to restore my spirit; that spirit which was consumed with joy during the years I spent at his side. Looking back on it all, I remember the wonderful days when I would become speechless at the beauty of his rosy face, which was the outer manifestation of his burning heart, absorbed with love for Jesus and Mary. How beautiful it was to go into his room and find him in ecstasy, how beautiful it was to see him leave his heavenly Visitors; ready to share his gifts with souls, through the sacrament of penance; how beautiful it was to go to his confessional box; put my arm under his, and walk back with him to his cell where he would never stop thanking me for helping him in his old-age. No, Padre, it is I who must thank you for allowing me this great privilege, and for opening up to my human eyes, a little bit of Heaven in my priestly life. What can I say? Thank you, Padre Pio!

PERSISTENT ANGEL

"And the angel of the Lord called to Abraham a second time from heaven..." (Gen 22:15)

Padre Paolino da Casacalenda, in his book* "Le Mie Memorie Intorno A Padre Pio", describes how, during the time he spent with Padre Pio, he became quite confidential with him and consequently, sometimes questioned him on the capabilities of his Guardian Angel. Often, Padre Pio would not answer his questions directly, as he evidently found it embarrassing to explain to his confréres the details of his supernatural experiences,

* - In Italian only.

but sometimes, Padre Paolino received concrete replies confirming how he loved his little Angel and how Padre Pio, in turn, was loved by his "companion".

On one occasion, when they were alone in the Friary, during the time when Padre Pio was ill, Padre Paolino knew that he needed help, especially during the night when he perspired a lot. On the other hand, he knew that he couldn't help Padre Pio very much as, overwhelmed by his heavy work load, as soon as he hit the bed, he would fall sound asleep and not wake up until the morning. However, one evening. Padre Paolino went into our beloved Padre's room saying: "Listen Father, I will gladly come to help you tonight, especially when you perspire, but if you want me to wake up, send me your Guardian Angel." As he didn't receive a reply, Padre Paolino added: "Do we agree?" And the answer: "Fine!" Padre Paolino returned to his room and, it goes without saying, went fast asleep, forgetting Padre Pio, his Guardian Angel, and the reasons for which he should arise during the night.

It was probably mid-night when he awoke from his peaceful sleep and he immediately thought of Padre Pio. However, regardless of this abrupt awakening during the night, the following morning he woke up realizing that he had not done his duty at all. Later on, he went into Padre Pio's room explaining what had happened to him and he added: "Padre Pio, what was the purpose of your Guardian Angel's coming to wake me up when, in the end, he left me to sleep again? If he comes tonight, he must wake me up in such a way that I get up out of bed!" He repeated these same words to Padre Pio that night before he retired, but, even on the next occasion, although he felt himself being woken up, and in a stronger manner than the night before, he immediately went to sleep again and the following morning, found himself in bed, just as the morning before.

On the third night, he went to greet Padre Pio and requested that, either his Guardian Angel should well and truly waken him up or, leave him in peace so that he should not have any scruples the following morning. It was about 1.30 that night when he felt something wake him up so definitely that he immediately jumped out of bed and, running to Padre Pio's room, asked him what he needed. And Padre Pio said: "I am soaked with perspiration. Please help me to change as I cannot do it alone". It is to be noted here that Padre Paolino arrived just in time to be of help to Padre Pio. One could say that it was purely coincidental, but, considering that Padre Pio had said that he would send his Guardian Angel to wake his aid up, it is beyond question that our little friend proved himself useful once again.

ANGEL OF ALL TRADES

"Are they not all ministering spirits sent forth to serve..."
(Heb 1:14)

The same service which Padre Pio's Guardian Angel performed for me, he also performed for Padre Pio himself every morning, and this can be verified by the venerable Padre's own words as he wrote to Father Agostino: "... At night when I close my eyes the veil is lifted and I see Paradise open up before me; and, gladdened by this vision, I sleep with a smile of sweet beatitude on my lips and a perfectly tranquil countenance, waiting for the little companion of my childhood (Guardian Angel) to come to waken me, so that we may sing together the morning praises to the Beloved of our hearts." (Letters I No. 100)

Padre Pio's very useful little Angel was often sent by him to those in need. In a letter to Padre Benedetto dated 28 July 1913, he says: "The Lord knows what tears I shed for you especially since I know what you are suffering. I never begin to pray without presenting you to our most sweet Jesus. I have never ascended the altar without recommending you fervently to the heavenly Father. On the 20th. of this month, I offered the Holy Sacrifice for you. My good Guardian Angel knows this and I have entrusted him many times with the delicate task of coming to console you." (Letters I No. 141)

However, as we have already seen, there were times when his Angel did not obey so quickly, but it seems he had good reason, as the following story told by Father Lino Barbato will point out: "Padre Pio was more tired than usual and could not rest. I suggested to him: 'Padre, if you recommend yourself to your Guardian Angel, he will make sure that you rest.' He

"... Near us is a celestial spirit, who, from the cradle to the tomb, does not leave us for an instant."

Padre Pio

The author, Father Alessio, with Padre Pio. Father Alessio was constantly at Padre Pio's side for almost six years.

"When you cannot come to me, send me your Guardian Angel. He can take a message from you to me and I will assist you as much as I can."

Padre Pio

"How beautiful it was to put my arm under his and walk with him back to his cell where he would never stop thanking me for helping him in his old-age."
The vast crowd presses itself on Padre Pio as Father Alessio (the author) escorts him to his cell.

replied: 'What if my Angel says that we have to suffer?' "

Padre Pio later on confirmed this idea when he said: "The Angels envy us for one thing only; they cannot suffer for God."

He did not use these words lightly as, one day, after he had been attacked by the devils, his Angel appeared to him saying: "Thank Jesus who is treating you as one chosen to follow him up the steep ascent of Calvary; soul confided by Jesus to my care, I behold with joy and deep emotion this behaviour of Jesus towards you. Do you perhaps think I should be so happy if I did not see you ill-treated like this? I who in holy charity greatly desire your good, rejoice more and more to see you in this state. Jesus permits these assaults of the devil because his compassion makes you dear to him and he wants you to resemble him in the torments in the desert, in the Garden and on the Cross." (Letters I No. 113)

Without a doubt, Padre Pio did have an "Angel of all Trades"; one who gave messages to others; one who consoled, woke him up and gave him counsel, but much more besides as we will see in the following pages.

THE GLOBE - TROTTING ANGEL

"... *And a messenger has been sent amongst the nations...*"
(Obad 1:1)

Whilst gathering together all the various information on Padre Pio's Guardian Angel, I must admit that my sympathy began to rest, almost entirely with this little "companion". The reason being, that throughout all the stories, he never seemed to have a moment's rest and I discovered that his zone of activity did not only encompass his charge's homeland (evidently he had no national prejudice!), but, on the contrary, he was prepared to travel on a much wider scale. Padre Gabriele Bove's story will help to clarify this point: Towards the end of a Summer's day in 1956, after having prayed at length and after having blessed the people from the window of the old choir, Padre Pio left the chapel extremely tired. It seemed as if the hot day had weighed on him more heavily than usual. He walked majestically, leaning heavily on the arm of Padre Giambattista of Sant'Elia a Pianisi, and he looked like Saint Francis with the stigmata, suffering and coming down the mountain.

With great care, Padre Gabriele took his other arm saying: "Padre, how tired you are this evening!" He replied: "Yes, my son. I am really crushed by this excessive heat." Padre Gabriele continued: "Without a doubt, tonight's rest will do you good and also... we will ask your Guardian Angel to comfort you." What he said seemed so strange to Padre Pio that he stopped in his tracks and shouted: "But what are you saying?... He has to travel!" This was exactly what Padre Gabriele wanted to hear from him. Without waiting any longer, and hiding his surprise, he added: "Who, your Guardian Angel, Padre, has to travel around?" "Certainly", he replied. "I thought it best not to ask any more questions just then", remarked Padre Gabriele and he told me: "I was profoundly moved and reflected with joy that what was said about him and his Guardian Angel was indeed true." A little later, Padre Gabriele tactfully asked Padre Pio: "Padre, if your Angel has to go about rescuing sinners and comforting the sick, will you permit our two Guardian Angels to take his place?" But he replied: "No, never. Indeed it is right that each of your Angels stays with his charge." Both Padre Giambattista and Padre Gabriele agreed reluctantly with this and asking for Padre Pio's blessing, left him alone, but not before he lovingly placed his hands on their heads and, lowering his voice, smilingly said: "One never knows; supposing these Angels become jealous?" It was one of those witty remarks of his intended to turn their attention away from him. They were, however, convinced of the truth; his Angel was already getting ready to go around the world on a night mission. Padre Pio remained an alert sentinel in the night, praying for the sick and for sinners.

IN A PRISON CAMP

"When they had passed the first and the second guard, they came to the iron gate leading into the city" (Acts 12:10)

Was Padre Pio the only one who received practical help from his Guardian Angel, or was he perhaps one of the very few who realized just who it was helping him? Many stories have come my way of people who, having prayed to the Angels for help in difficult situations, received the help they needed, in an extraordinary way. To those without faith, or even to those with great faith, it would simply be a wonderful co-incidence, but to others, it could be the work of the ever-available Angels. Well it could quite possibly be so as they looked after Padre Pio in times of great difficulty. Perhaps the only difference is that he, by a special grace, actually saw these celestial creatures, whilst we cannot. But that does not mean that they are not working just the same. Let me tell you a few stories:

In her book "A PRISONER AND YET", C. Boom tells of the angelic emergency service in a Nazi prison camp: "Upon entering the camp we had to surrender, not only our clothes, but also our medicines. But we were allowed to keep a few toilet articles. My small bottle of "Davitamon", a liquid vitamin compound, was then about half full. I set it down on the table and the woman who was checking us in said: 'That is also a toilet article.' She put it back in my bag with her own hands and I was very happy about it. Vitamin deficiency was the greatest hazard amongst the prisoners. From the very first day, I gave everyone sleeping around me a couple of drops of "Davitamon" every day. I gave it to as many as thirty persons at a time, but the little bottle continued to yield its drops. This went on for six or eight weeks until the women no longer asked me: 'Do you still have some "Davitamon" but, 'Do you still have any oil from the cruse of the widow of Zerephath?'

"They were right in calling it that, for, as the jar of meal never finished, neither did my "Davitamon". Then one day, my friend, who worked in the hospital, brought me a jar of vitamins; I believe it was brewers yeast. 'Give this to all the women around you', she said. 'But do not tell anyone that I gave it to you.' So I gave each woman enough to last her for a week.

"That evening, I said to my sister Betsie: 'I am going to give you "Davitamon" too, as long as it lasts', but not a drop came out of the bottle. The miracle was no longer necessary.

"The bag of vitamins was also blessed. There always seemed to be enough, until one evening someone asked me: 'Do you still have some vitamins?' 'No', I said. I'm very sorry but it's all gone.' I still had a tiny bit left but wanted to keep it for Betsie. Now, I confessed to her: 'That really showed that I was lacking in faith. I should have been more confident and given her the last little bit.' Scarcely had I uttered the words when I saw my friend from the hospital approaching and she actually had another bagful of vitamins with her. It was a great miracle. Vitamins were hard to get throughout the entire camp. Even if a doctor felt they were necessary for some patient he wanted to favour, he still would be unable to procure them. It really is not out of place to speak of the miracle of the vitamins."

Could it possibly be true that in every miracle, or even in the case of a lucky co-incidence, that it was an Angel sent to administer to a soul in need? C. Boom tells us another story of the time when both she and her sister entered the dreaded concentration camp. Relating the horrible indignities and privations they suffered, she writes: "Together we entered the terrifying building. At the table were women who took away all our possessions. Everyone had to undress completely and then go to a room where her hair was clipped short. I asked a guard, who was busy checking the possessions of the new arrivals, if I might use the toilet. She pointed to a door to the showers. Betsie stayed close beside me all the time. Suddenly, I had an inspiration. 'Quick, take off your woolen underwear', I whispered to her. I rolled it up with mine and laid it in a corner with my little Bible. The spot was alive with cockroaches but I didn't worry about that. I felt wonderfully relieved and happy...

"We hurried back to the row of women waiting to be undressed. A little later, after we had our showers and put on our shirts and shabby dresses, I hid the roll of underwear and my Bible under my dress. It did bulge out obviously but I prayed: 'Lord, cause now thine Angels to surround me and let them not be transparent today, for the guards must not see me.' I felt perfectly at ease. Calmly I passed the guards. The woman just in front of me had hidden a woolen vest under her dress; it was taken from her. They let me pass, for they did not see me. Betsie, right behind me, was searched.

"But outside, awaited another danger. On each side of the door were women who looked over everyone for the second time. They felt over the body of each one who passed. I knew they would not see for the Angels were still surrounding me. I was not even surprised when they passed me by, but within me rose the jubilant cry: 'O Lord, if you answer my prayer, I can face even this camp unafraid.' "

She passed through with the help of thc Angels whom she had asked to help her.

This story I related to you for a specific purpose. When speaking to many people about the Guardian Angels, the comments have often been as follows: "Oh, well, Padre Pio was a very holy man, very close to our Lord wasn't he? or, "I'm just a poor sinner, why should my Angel do anything to help me?" Yes, Padre Pio was a very holy man, but I believe our Angels work well for each one of us too if we only have faith, and I hope that the story just told, reveals this.

In conclusion, for my part, I would like

to express my own gratitude to my Guardian Angel whose help I have often experienced, particularly in times of difficulties and trials. The conviction that I am protected by a prince of the heavenly army, fills me with reverence, devotion and confidence. Our prayers for his help are the clearest and best expression of this confidence, which should remain with us throughout our lives. And I end with the words of His Holiness Pope Pius XI, who said: "... (Devotion to my Guardian Angel) was impressed in my mind early in life by my mother, as soon as I was able to understand it. This supported me in all the things I have accomplished in life, with the help of God's grace, and it will certainly be my support in the remaining part of my life which God will grant me."

THE HEAVENLY POSTMAN

"... Go, you swift messengers..."
(Is 18:2)

One of the most common responsibilities of the Angels, as stated in the fourteenth verse of the first chapter of Hebrews, is that of messenger "sent out". This seems to be particularly true of their actions as recorded in the Old Testament. They were God's "special delivery" messengers. Let us examine these heavenly messengers a little more carefully:

During his life time, Padre Pio formed an army which he called his "Spiritual Children". This means that many people put themselves under his spiritual direction and guidance, thus they could participate in the fruits of his prayers and sufferings. Usually he would accept those who requested this honour, however, whilst at his side, I heard him deny this benefit to a few with the words: "You must become a son of God first, then come back and I will accept you as my spiritual child, but don't let me lose face."

One day, while Padre Pio was passing through the Saint Francis room, he was approached by a young man who asked him if he could become his spiritual child. Padre Pio's brief reply was: "Yes!" However, the young man continued: "But Father, next week I leave for America where I will live with my family", and Padre Pio said: "Do you think I cannot go there and slap you if you don't lead a good life?"

Once a person was accepted as Padre Pio's spiritual child, he would never abandon them, no matter what danger they were in. Even if he did not visit them personally, they would receive his help through his Guardian Angel.

Cecil Humphrey-Smith, a well known

gentleman from England, is Padre Pio's spiritual child. Whilst in Italy, during the time Padre Pio was alive, Cecil had a car crash and was very seriously injured. A friend of his, seeing him in such a bad condition afterwards, went to the Post Office and sent a telegram to Padre Pio requesting his prayers for the injured Cecil. When he presented the telegram at the desk, the man gave him back a telegram from Padre Pio assuring his prayers for Cecil Humphrey-Smith's recovery.

It was some months before Cecil was in good enough shape to travel again, but immediately he had recovered he made tracks for San Giovanni Rotondo. On this occasion, both Cecil and his friend met Padre Pio and they thanked him for his prayers. At the same time, they were curious to know how he came to know about the accident and how a telegram had arrived in such a short space of time. In response to their demand, Padre Pio, in his humoristic way said: "Do you think the Angels go as slowly as the planes?"

God had given him the light to see his spiritual child in danger of death and, as usual, he sent his Guardian Angel to assure his prayers and protection.

Here at Our Lady of Grace Friary, we produce a magazine called "The Voice of Padre Pio", in which we publish information on the work going on at the shrine. This magazine is a mine of information on the life of Padre Pio and arrives six times a year in the homes of devotees throughout the world. The arrival of this magazine usually serves to brighten the day of those who receive it, but in some cases it has a very special significance... I receive a lot of English mail from all parts of the world and often people tell me how glad they are to receive it. On a number of occasions I was told of cases where a subscriber was feeling very depressed due to family problems or difficulties of some sort. Knowing that Padre Pio had always told them to send him their Guardian Angel, the ever-ready Angel was sent, and within a short time they found "The Voice" in their letter box! Nothing would convince these devotees . that it was not their Guardian Angel who delivered it in time of need, acting on Padre Pio's instructions. The Bible tells us that the Angels act as messengers "sent out", and Padre Pio told us that they go faster than the planes so there is no need to doubt it.

"... GO LITTLE FRIEND AND FIND
THAT SPECIAL ONE
AND WARM HIS SOUL WITH WORDS OF FRIENDSHIP-
- THEN YOUR TASK'S WELL DONE."
(ANONYMOUS)

THE ANGELIC PROCESSION

"... And behold the angels of God were ascending and descending on it." (Gen 28:13)

Being at Padre Pio's side for almost six years, I clearly understood how many people sent their Guardian Angels to him, when they wished him to receive some message or to be remembered in his prayers. In fact, passing through the crowd with him, as I did every day, I often heard it said: "Father, as I will not be able to come to see you again, what should I do if I need your prayers?" And Padre Pio would reply: "If you cannot come to me, send me your Guardian Angel. He can take a message from you to me and I will assist you as much as I can."

What a wonderful way to keep in touch with his spiritual children! What a marvellous "invention" with which to communicate with the world. Not the usual means such as a letter, a telegram; not by train or plane or any other man-made means of communication; but a supernatural one, a spirit, an Angel who flies faster than any of these modern means. The words: "Send me your Guardian Angel", were regularly heard from Padre Pio's lips.

One day, I was sitting by his side on the verandah near his room and it was about 2.30 in the afternoon. All the friars had, by then, retired to their rooms to take a "siesta", so the area was deserted. I saw Padre Pio fingering his rosary and there was such a peace and calm around him that I felt encouraged to approach him and ask some questions. During those years, I used to receive many letters from people asking me to seek Padre Pio's advice on a problem of some sort. I opened a letter and, turning to Padre Pio said: "Father, Mrs. B.R. seeks your counsel about her job.

She has a good job but another firm is offering her a better one and a better salary, which would mean a much easier life for her. What do you think she should do?" To my surprise, I did not receive an answer from him but, rather, a scolding: "Come on, my son, leave me alone. Don't you see that I am very busy?" "Strange", I thought. "He is sitting down fingering his rosary and he says he is busy." While I remained totally silent thinking it was not true that he was busy, Padre Pio turned to me and said: "Didn't you see all those Guardian Angels going backwards and forwards from my spiritual children bringing messages from them?" Not surprised at his words I retorted: "Father, I have not seen even one Guardian Angel, but I believe you because you tell people every day to send you theirs."

The unending procession of Guardian Angels to Padre Pio did not cease with the setting sun. On the contrary; at night time, I would help him to lie down for his short sleep and then, position myself on the armchair in his room, waiting for Padre

Pellegrino to come on duty and assist him. Whilst waiting, I always heard Padre Pio reciting the rosary, but very often, I heard him disrupt the recitation with disjointed sentences like: "Tell her I will pray for her", or "Tell her that I will storm Heaven for her sake", or "Tell him that I will knock at the heart of Jesus for this grace", or "Tell him that he will be present in my Mass", or "Tell her that Our Lady will not refuse her this grace". These and other similar remarks were quite the usual, but I never heard any questions! I realized later that Padre Pio was giving answers to the various Guardian Angels, when a few people wrote to me saying that, for some reason, they had sent their Guardian Angels to him and, almost immediately, they received the favour they requested.

Mrs. A.P. wrote to me and said: "Father Alessio, the other night I was very sick with stomach-ache. I was all alone and as the vomiting was very bad, desperation overwhelmed me as I felt that I would die. I had nobody to turn to but, being a spiritual child of Padre Pio, I sent him my Guardian

Angel and immediately, the pain stopped. I felt better than I had ever felt before."

Mr. D.C. wrote to me also, and said: "Please extend my sincere thanks to Padre Pio for the wonderful grace he obtained for me last night. I was with some friends in a restaurant and we enjoyed a lovely dinner. At about mid-night, one of them suggested that we break into a jewellery shop. The others agreed and, so as not to lose face, I did too; really I didn't want to. In that moment, I thought of my wonderful wife and lovely children but I felt trapped in the plan. When I realized my friends were determined to do the job, in which I would be involved, I immediately thought of Padre Pio and mentally sent him my Guardian Angel saying: 'Tell Padre Pio to come and rescue me.' Hardly had I uttered the words when a police car passed, and scared, the gang dispersed. With a deep sigh of relief, I made my way home with the words: 'Thank you, Padre Pio, and you too, my good Guardian Angel.' "

Do we realize just how useful our Angels can be? In these modern times when the existence of hell, the devil and even the good Lord himself is doubted, isn't it rather extraordinary to hear that, not so long ago, there lived a priest who used these very creatures, whose existence we perhaps doubt, to run errands for him, to protect people in danger, to convert sinners and even to translate other languages? Was it just he who had a wonderful Angel? Indeed he did have an extraordinary one but if we believc in Padre Pio's words at all, then we must accept the fact that each one of us has at his side, a friendly "companion"who is ever-ready to obey our commands and help us in whatever way he can. The above letters from various people form a very minute part of the many thousands of letters which I received from people telling me of how their Guardian Angels work for them, and we will deal with some more later on.

PANIS ANGELICUS

"... He gave them bread from heaven:
men ate the bread of angels."
(Ps 77:24-25)

A long time ago, before Padre Pio was even dreamt of, the Angels were busily working in San Giovanni Rotondo, and this story dates back to the years when the Friary had been constructed only a short time:

*"A lot of snow had fallen that year, so much, in fact, that the door of the church and of the Friary became entrenched, so that the friar who usually went to beg for

---

* - Taken from "San Giovanni Rotondo, Nella luce Del Francescanesimo" By Francesco Morcaldi.

food, could not go to provide for the needs of his brothers. Already, all the bread and beans had been consumed, and, having no hope of human aid, they turned to the Lord. Towards evening, four young men of gentle countenance, one with bread, another with wine, and the others with various kinds of food, appeared at the door. As there was nobody in the Friary who knew them, the brother doorman asked them where they had come from and who had been the alms-giver, in order that they could thank him. And they said: "Thank the Lord who does not abandon his faithful servants in their necessity." And, having said that, they immediately left.

"A few days passed and, the villagers, amazed that the friars had not come to seek alms from the people, and believing that, because of the snow, they would be found in dire need, opened the road to the Friary. They discovered that a few days earlier they had been very badly in need, but then, because of the help of the four young men, they were saved from extreme shortage. When the people returned to the village and explained what had happened, a diligent search was made to find out who the benefactors could have been, but they discovered nothing at all. Knowing that the friars could not have received alms from other villages, because they were so far away, and the snow was so high, they realized that it had been a miracle and were convinced that it had been the work of the Angels, in the form of young men, who had provided for the necessities of the devoted poor of Jesus Christ."

At about the same time, a similar incident occurred at the Friary when brother Antonio Da Toro was the alms seeker. As he had such great charity towards the poor, he would often return to the Friary without any bread, because he never refused anyone who begged from him. One day, the Superior severely reprimanded him for this, but he answered contentedly: "Father, I knew there was no bread in the Friary, and that you had sent me out to beg for it, but when I was coming back some poor people came around me, and I had not got the heart to deny them the charity that they were asking in the name of God, Who became poor for us. But, do not doubt; the Lord has provided bread for us too. Let's go and see it." The Superior went with him and was amazed to see, in the larder, a vast amount of bread, which was still steaming as if it had just been taken out of the oven.

Evidently, as in the case previously mentioned, the "ministering spirits" had obeyed the Lord's commands and had, once again, provided for those in need.

All this happened quite some time ago, but, during the time when Padre Pio was alive, I personally was involved in a little incident which concerned the "Bread of Angels". Let me tell you: "In 1959 I was assigned by the Superiors as Sacristan in Our Lady of Grace Friary. At that time, Padre Pio used to say Mass at 5 A.M. and Holy Communion was not distributed during that Mass, but afterwards. As soon as Padre Pio came into the sacristy after Mass, I would go out to distribute Holy Communion to the many people in the church. There was always a rush to be first at the altar rails so that one could receive and then move into the little church, where Padre Pio would hear confessions.

One day, there were so many people receiving that the big ciborium which I held in my hands was soon emptied completely. While another priest continued to distribute Holy Communion to those people left at the altar rails, I went back to the altar and started to purify the ciborium. After I had taken away the small particles, I poured some water into it and washed it well, then I took a purificator to dry it. I was just finished this and was about to put the cover on it when I saw, on my right side, a Host, in mid-air, heading for the ciborium, and it dropped in. Automatically, my head jerked towards the right, but there was no one there! The other priest was still at the altar rails. I was a little shocked, to say the least, and when my brother friar returned from the altar rails, I took the Host and put it into his ciborium.

Later on during the day, I told Padre Pio of my experience and when he had heard the full story, he said: "Be more careful and don't rush when you distribute Holy Communion. Thank your Guardian Angel who did not let Jesus fall on the floor." This remark of Padre Pio's brought to mind a similar incident when one of my brother friars said to him: "Father, our eyes are not so good that we can see any small particles of the Sacred Species which fall down while we distribute Holy Communion." Padre Pio replied: "What do you think the Angels do around the altar?" With this remark we understood that no matter how small a particle falls, the Angels are ever-ready to collect it and bring it back to the ciborium.

How many things happen in this world of which we humans remain completely unaware? How many times have our Guardian Angels saved us from some accident or prevented us from committing some sin? And when a mother, looking at her little infant smiling, says: "He is smiling at the angels", does she really believe it? Well, why not. A number of the Archangels said to Magdalen of the Cross:

"I am assured in this moment by my Guardian Angel that a letter of yours is on its way to me."

Padre Pio

"Be more careful and don't rush when you distribute Holy Communion. Thank your Guardian Angel who did not let Jesus fall on the floor."

Padre Pio

"Thank Jesus who is treating you as one chosen to follow him closely up the steep ascent of Calvary."

Guardian Angel.

Fr. Alessio Parente holding a crucifix, which Padre Pio kisses with immense love.

"An innocent human soul is even more beautiful than an Angel in all his glory." Is not a little infant an innocent human soul? And, if so, surely he would be visited by the angels. I, for my part, am absolutely convinced of it.

Send Your Angel To Holy Mass

O holy Angel at my side,
Go to the church for me,
Kneel in my place at Holy Mass
Where I desire to be.

At Offertory, in my stead,
Take all I am and own,
And place it as a sacrifice
Upon the altar throne.

At holy consecration's bell,
Adore with seraph's love
My Jesus hidden in the Host
Come down from heav'n above.

Then pray for those I dearly love,
And those who cause me grief,
That Jesus' Blood may cleanse all hearts
And suffering souls relieve.

And when the priest Communion takes,
Oh, bring my Lord to me,
That His sweet Heart may rest on mine
And I His temple be.

Pray that this Sacrifice Divine
May mankind's sins efface;
Then bring me Jesus' blessing home -
The pledge of every grace.

Anonymous

THE ANGEL STAYS AT HOME

"Do not depart from here, I pray thee..." (Judg 6:18)

Father Joseph Pius Martin, who is a member of the community here at Our Lady of Grace Friary, and who spent some years looking after Padre Pio, told me the following story: Martha moved to San Giovanni Rotondo from Switzerland and attended faithfully Padre Pio's Mass and Benediction during the day, and his blessing at night. Customarily, he gave his last blessing of the day from the window of his cell; he would appear there and bless all the people gathered below.

One day, something came up and Martha had to go to Rome. That evening,

Padre Pio went to the window of his cell to give the usual blessing. One of the friars who assisted him opened the window and Padre Pio started to wave to the people below. Suddenly, he froze, as he appeared to look at, and listen to, someone whom the friars with him could not see. Padre Pio then turned to the friar who had opened the window and said: "Where is Martha tonight?" The reply he received was that Martha had had to go to Rome, so Padre Pio continued with the blessing and all was well.

When Martha returned, one of the friars said to her: "You sent your Guardian Angel for the evening blessing didn't you?" Martha was surprised but had to admit that she did. It had been only too obvious to those priests who accompanied Padre Pio on this occasion. They knew Martha would miss the blessing so, seeing Padre Pio listening to the unseen personage, they guessed that she had sent him her Guardian Angel.

Father 'Joseph recounted to me another story: Father Dominic Meyer lived with Padre Pio for several years after having been stationed in Rome. He did not give much credence to the stories of Padre Pio conversing with the Guardian Angels. One morning, he met Padre Pio in the hallway of the Friary and he noticed that he was very tired. He asked him why, and the reply he received was: "The Guardian Angels came to me all night long and they didn't give me much chance to rest." Of course, Father Dominic's opinion of Padre Pio's conversing with the Angels soon changed after that!

Another similar story was referred to Rev. Father Clement Noef by Mary Pyle, when he was a sergeant in the U.S. Army Air Corps: Two girls, neighbours, spent the night together at one of their houses. Like all young girls, they did a lot of talking after they went to bed. The conversation started on Padre Pio. You see, they were about that age when religion begins to make an impression and they had come to realize that they had a famous person living in their town who apparently had a special relationship with his Angel. They discussed the fact that anyone of us could send his Guardian Angel to Padre Pio with whatever message he wished. This was too good an opportunity to miss, so, one little girl said: "I am going to send my Guardian Angel to Padre Pio to ask him to cure my uncle Fred", the other replied: "I am going to send my Guardian Angel to Padre Pio to ask him to cure my cousin", and so it went.

The next morning after Mass (it was the days when the girls could go into the Sacristy behind the main altar), they went back to get Padre Pio's blessing and were very surprised and hurt to find that he was angry with them. When they asked why, he said to them: "You kept me awake all night. First you sent me your Guardian Angel to cure your uncle Fred", he said pointing to the culprit, "and then you sent yours asking that your cousin be cured", he said to the other. "And you kept it up all night long", he continued, "I didn't get any sleep!"

Was Padre Pio really annoyed with these two young ladies, or was he simply pointing out to them the fact that their

Guardian Angels did really do as they were told and came to him all night long? I must hasten to agree with the latter, not simply because I knew Padre Pio very well, but also because I have been told another story which seems to point out that, he welcomed the Angels not twelve, but twenty-four hours a day:

Carmela Marocchino came to San Giovanni Rotondo in 1937 and stayed in Mary Pyle's house until 1942, when she left and moved to Pietrelcina. After the war, she returned once again for a time until, finally, in 1952, she settled down completely with Mary and acted as her housekeeper. Naturally, she came to know Padre Pio very well and confessed regularly to him. Often, as she was worried about travelling up to the Friary in bad weather, he would say to her: "Don't worry, the Angel of the Lord will go with you".

On one occasion, when she was feeling concerned over some problem or other, she wanted to send her Guardian Angel to Padre Pio. But, as at this time it was quite late at night, she decided not to, as she didn't want to disturb her spiritual father. When next she met Padre Pio, she told him what had happened and he said to her: "You may send your Guardian Angel any time of the day or night, as I am always happy to receive him".

So it would appear, that Padre Pio really was only telling the girls that their Angels did their work very well indeed, and of course, each time he said: "Send me your Guardian Angel", he meant at any time of the day or night. What a pleasure it must have been for him to see, not only his own Angel at his side, but also those of his spiritual children, as they appeared before his human eyes in all their celestial splendour.

ANGEL AT THE WHEEL

"... Get ready for the journey and good success to you both..."
(Tob 5:16)

A friend of mine, Mr. Piergiorgio Biavati, since gone to his heavenly reward, told me the following story: He was travelling from Florence to San Giovanni Rotondo in order to attend Padre Pio's Mass and go to confession to him. Due to the heavy traffic on the "Autostrada del sole" (Motorway), he lost a good deal of time. He had calculated being in San Giovanni Rotondo at sun-set, instead, at that time, he had only succeeded in reaching Naples. With his nerves in pieces and feeling very tired, he decided to make an overnight stop there and travel to San

Giovanni the following morning.

He stopped at a snack-bar on the "autostrada" and went in for a cup of coffee. Afterwards, he hung around for another few minutes and felt the urge to have another. Some time passed and he went to have a third cup! (Dear reader, if you would drink even one cup of our strong Italian coffee, you would be awake for three days and three nights!) Having finished the third cup, he felt so relaxed and wide awake that he decided to continue the journey and thus avoid an overnight stop, even though by then it was getting very dark.

Here I quote Mr. Biavati's own words: "I remember only one thing; I started the engine, put my hands on the wheel and after that, I have no recollection whatsoever! I don't remember any second of the three hours drive. Not only that, but when I reached the square in front of the Friary, someone shook me by the shoulder and said: 'Come on, now, take over!' " You can imagine his astonishment; he must have driven for about three hours, yet he could not remember so much as one single second of the whole journey. Gripped by fear, he went to park the car and have a rest before going up to the Friary to attend Padre Pio's Mass. After Mass he approached Padre Pio and said: "Father, I drove here from Naples but I don't remember driving my car at all." And Padre Pio smilingly replied: "Yes, you are right. You were sleeping all the way and my Guardian Angel was driving for you!"

The "little man" was lucky that he wasn't stopped by the police as I'm sure he didn't have a licence!!! But if he protected one person so well on a long journey, I think we should all remember to say that well known prayer as we set out, and perhaps the time is ripe for me to print that little prayer and to suggest to all my readers that they utter its beautiful words as often as they can:

Oh Angel of God, my Guardian
dear

To whom His love commits me here
Ever this day be at my side
To light and guard, to rule and guide.

Amen

WAKEFUL ANGEL

"And the angel who talked with me came again, and waked me, like a man that is awakened out of his sleep..."
(Zech 4:1)

"May God and his Angels protect you", wrote Mrs. Bower, U.S.A., "like our Guardian Angels protected us on the journey from Wyoming to Norristown." This reminded me of the time when I had indeed travelled in that direction and the story goes as follows: In 1978, whilst making a lecture tour in the U.S.A., I was invited to a meeting in a friend's house in Wyoming. Mrs. Bower and her friend offered to drive me there. Once I had reached the meeting, the time seemed to fly and, before I realized it, it was 12 midnight. So we climbed back into the car to make the long journey home. Mrs. Bower had driven the car to Wyoming and now she was behind the wheel again. I was quite tired and, being in the back seat, I went to sleep.

We were only 20 miles away from Norristown when, in my sleep, a voice insisted: "Wake up, wake up!" I opened my eyes and, looking ahead, I saw our car getting closer and closer to a truck at high speed. I thought that Mrs. Bower was going to overtake it but, seeing the car going towards the right, I realized that she was sleeping. "Mary, Mary!", I shouted, and at this stage the car was already touching the foot-path.

Hearing her name being shouted so suddenly, Mrs. Bower jumped up and quickly pushed the brake bringing the car to a sudden stop, thus avoiding hitting the rail of a bridge which was just ahead of us. It took a few minutes for us to recover from the shock but, before we started out again, we asked our individual Guardian Angels to bring us home safely. Let me assure you that I thanked my "companion" all the way for saving us from a sure death.

In case the reader is of the impression that every time I take a nap, my Guardian Angel comes to rouse me from my slumber, such is definitely not the case. These days, I don't seem to find it any problem at all to shake off the "sand-man". Perhaps it is because I have, after Padre Pio's suggestion, invested in a new alarm-clock, the noise of which would surely waken the dead, not to mention the living! In fact, a friend of mine who came to my room recently, said that Big Ben couldn't "hold a candle" to it! Even at that, I regularly beat my alarm-clock to it and come down the stairs to my little office to do some work before the daily procession of visitors begins. (No, not the Angels!) It is not for nothing that I got the nick-name "the man who wants everything done yesterday!"

INVISIBLE COMPANION

"Give heed to him (Angel) and hearken to his voice..."
(Ex 23:21)

Padre Pio's spiritual guidance of souls was mostly done through the help and direction of his Guardian Angel: *"I am assured in this moment by my Guardian Angel", he wrote to Raffaelina Cerase, a spiritual child of his, "that a letter of yours is on its way to me. I am assured that this letter will cause me acute suffering. What can have happened to you? My God! It

---

* - Letters II No. 29.

* - Volume II of Padre Pio's letters is in Italian only at present.

seems to me a thousand years before I can receive this letter of yours. In the meantime, console yourself, because, although I ignore whatever misadventure has befallen you, I want you to know that it is Jesus who wished to make a present of this to you..." Finally, when he received the letter, he replied: "The fact has confirmed the announcement (of the Guardian Angel). Deo Grazias. Your letter dated the 21st. of this month has arrived. I read it and I cannot hold back the tears for the sad news it contains. Nevertheless, I resign myself and give thanks to the Lord knowing that this illness is desired by Jesus, not as a punishment but to sanctify your spirit." (Letters II No. 30)

On 25 October 1914, Padre Pio wrote once again to Raffaelina: "You tell me that in the midst of the sufferings that oppress you, you often turn to me in your thoughts and you call me. Well, your good Guardian Angel sometimes transmits these necessities of yours and then I, in my unworthiness, always do my duty with Jesus, recommending you to his Fatherly goodness." (Letters II No. 30)

In a letter of 17 December 1914, Padre Pio encourages Raffaelina Cerase not to forget her Guardian Angel: "Offer to the glory of His Divine Majesty the rest you are about to take, (she was struck down with cancer of the breast at this time) and never forget the Guardian Angel who is always with you, never leaving you for whatever wrong you might do. Oh, the ineffable goodness of this our good Guardian Angel! How many times, alas!, I have made him cry for not having wanted to comply with his wishes, which were also God's. May this our most faithful friend free us from further disloyalty." (Letters II No. 41)

On 20 April 1915, Padre Pio writes a real gem on the kindness, goodness, sincerity and loyalty of the Guardian Angel: "Oh Raffaelina, what a consolation it is to know one is always in the care of a celestial spirit, who does not abandon us (how admirable) even when we disgust God! How sweet is this great truth for the believer! Who, then, does the devout soul fear who tries to love Jesus, having always close by such a great warrior? Oh, was he not one of the many who, together with the Angel Saint Michael, up there in the Empyrean, defended the honour of God against Satan and against all the other rebellious spirits, and finally reduced them to perdition and bound them in hell?

"Well, know that he is still powerful against Satan and his satellites; his charity has not diminished, nor will he ever fail in defending us. Develop the beautiful habit of always thinking of him; that near us is a celestial spirit, who, from the cradle to the tomb, does not leave us for an instant; guides us, protects us as a friend, a brother; will always be a consolation to us especially in our saddest moments.

"Know, oh Raffaelina, that this good Angel prays for you; offers to God all the good works you accomplish; your holy and pure desires. In the hours when you seem to be alone and abandoned, do not complain of not having a friendly soul to whom you can unburden yourself and in whom you can confide your sorrows. For pity's sake, do not forget this invisible companion, always present to listen to you; always ready to console you.

"Oh delicious intimacy, oh blessed company! Oh if all men could understand this great gift that God, in His excess of love for man, assigned to us; this celestial spirit. Often remember his presence; you must fix on him the eyes of your soul; thank him; pray to him; he is so refined, so sensitive. Respect him; be in constant fear of offending the purity of his gaze.

"Invoke often this Guardian Angel, this benevolent Angel and repeat the beautiful prayer: 'Oh Angel of God' (etc.)...* What will be, oh my dear Raffaelina, the consolation when, at the moment of death, your soul will see this Angel, so good, who accompanied you through life and was so liberal in maternal care. Oh may this sweet thought make you grow always more fond of the Cross of Jesus, this being also what your good Angel wants. May the desire to

---

* - As on page 108.

see this inseparable companion arouse in you that charity which incites you to leave this body quickly.

"Oh what a holy and salutary thought it is to want to see this our good Angel. It is this thought which should make us want to leave this dark prison in which we are bound. Oh, Raffaelina, where do my thoughts fly to now...? Treat this dear little Angel, I do not say as a friend, but as one of the family. And, to tell you the truth, this little Angel does not seem to be the least little bit offended by my treatment of him. How dear and how good he is." (Letters II No. 64)

These words of Padre Pio to Raffaelina echo the words of the Holy Father Pope Pius XI, when, addressing a group of children from all parts of Italy he said: "Never forget your life companion. Show him reverence for his presence, for his loyalty and for his good will and have great confidence in his protection." The Holy Father, every day of his life, repeatedly called on his Angel for help, particulary in times of difficulty and trials.

Obviously for Padre Pio, after Jesus and Mary came his Guardian Angel, who played a very important role in his sanctification and mission. He and his Guardian Angel are so closely linked with one another that it is impossible to separate them. His Angel knew how to guide, enlighten and direct him along the difficult path to sanctity, and Padre Pio was a very docile instrument in his hands.

Devout Invocations of the Guardian Angel

Lord have mercy on us etc.

God the Father of Heaven,
[have mercy on us.

God the Son, Redeemer of men,
[have mercy on us.

God the Holy Spirit,
[have mercy on us.

Holy Spirit, one God,
[have mercy on us.

Holy Mary Queen of Heaven,
[pray for us.

Holy Angel my Guardian,
[pray for us.

Holy Angel my protector in all dangers,
[pray for us.

Holy Angel, my defence in all afflictions,
[pray for us.

Holy Angel, my most faithful lover,
[pray for us.

Holy Angel my preceptor,
[pray for us.

Holy Angel my guide,
[pray for us.

Holy Angel witness of all my actions,
[pray for us.

Holy Angel, my helper in all my difficulties,
[pray for us.

Holy Angel, my advocate,
[pray for us.

Holy Angel lover of chastity,
[pray for us.

Holy Angel lover of innocence,
[pray for us.

Holy Angel most obedient to God,
[pray for us.

Holy Angel director of my soul,
[pray for us.

Holy Angel model of purity,
[pray for us.

Holy Angel, model of docility,
[pray for us.

Holy Angel my counseller in doubt,
[pray for us.

Holy Angel my guardian through life,
[pray for us.

Holy Angel my shield at the hour of death,
[pray for us.

Lamb of God have mercy on us etc.

Prayer: O God who, with unspeakable providence, vouchsafest to send thy Angels to be our Guardians, mercifully grant, that we Thy suppliants, may be always defended by their protection and enjoy their eternal society, through Jesus Christ, Your Son, Our Lord, who lives and reigns with you and the Holy Spirit, one God forever and ever, Amen.

(For private devotion)

Prayer to the Guardian Angel

O Holy Angel, whom God, by the effect of His goodness and tender regard for my welfare, has charged with the care of my conduct, who supports me when I am discouraged and continually obtains for me new favours, I return thee profound thanks and conjure thee, most amiable protector, to continue thy charitable care and defence of me against the malignant attacks of all my enemies. Keep me at a distance from all occasions of sin. Obtain for me the grace of hearkening attentively to the holy inspirations and of faithfully reducing them to practise. Protect me in all the temptations and trials of this life, but more especially at the hour of my death, and do not leave me until you have conducted me into the presence of my Creator, in the mansions of everlasting happiness. Amen.

AN ANGEL SANG

"Praise him, all his angels, praise him, all his host!" (Ps. 148:2)

The idea of my writing a book on Padre Pio and the Angels was conceived some time ago but it was quite a while before I got down to actually doing it. When eventually I did get down to it, I found the going hard and began to get very discouraged thinking that perhaps Padre Pio did not really want me to write it at all. Finally, on a day when the waste-paper basket looked very tempting, I decided to put it off for another while and dejectedly made my way to the mail box to answer some letters. I picked up the first letter from the pile and began to read... It told of the extraordinary experience of Mrs. A. Ahrens from the U.S.A. and it concerned the Angels. "Could this be a little bit of encouragement from above?", I wondered. I was amazed, so with renewed fervour I once again tackled the book and this time things seemed to go very well. I now publish Mrs. Ahrens letter to show you why it meant so much to me and I would like to add that the happening was witnessed by four people, one of whom was a priest:

"My husband, Milo, was very ill and suffering great pain. His body was almost completely consumed with cancer and his vision and hearing were severely impaired. About two weeks before the Lord took him to Himself, a beautiful thing happened. Our nephew, Rev. Fr. Frank Bognanno and our eldest daughter were visiting Milo in the nursing home where he had been bedridden for three months. Milo was a very deeply religious man and loved praying and singing. Fr. Frank lead us in prayer as we knelt around his bed, and then into singing songs of praise. My eyes were closed as were those of the others present, our usual manner in prayer. We were singing the "Alleluia" and another male voice joined us in beautiful harmony. The door was open and I assumed that the voice, which was coming from my right side, was that of my son who had come to see his father. We sang several verses and were blessed by the peace and spiritual love surrounding us. When we finished our "Alleluia", I turned to greet my son and found nobody there! Tears started to roll down my cheeks; my daughter asked me if something was wrong; I could not explain the crying. Perhaps they were the gift of tears from being overwhelmed because somebody had been there. I had felt, heard and enjoyed something beautiful that I could not explain. In the course of conversation, we felt something extraordinary had happened. We had all heard the beautiful angelic voice and harmony. Milo then said that an Angel had been with us and sang the "Alleluia" in harmony. Our encounter with an Angel was beautiful and, for my beloved husband, Milo, this was only a token of what our Heavenly Father had prepared for him when a host of Angels would carry him before the throne of God to be forever in Heaven.

"This was a wonderful and timely experience because my husband passed away ten days after seeing the Angel. How precious to know our Guardian Angels are ever with us."

Did an Angel really come and visit Milo on his death bed? I can only remind the reader of Padre Pio's own words when he said to Raffaelina Cerase: "At the moment of death your soul will see this Angel, so good, who accompanied you through life and was so liberal in maternal care..." Do our individual Angels really visit us on our death beds? Do we accept Padre Pio's words? Then, if so, isn't it quite possible that Milo's Angel was with him as he approached death?

As we already know, it is one of the functions of the Angels to praise and glorify God, and in the Bible, we come across numerous occasions when they

"... They are the voices of Angels who are taking souls from Purgatory into Paradise."

Padre Pio

''Padre Pio had somebody translate the letters for him. It was, in fact, his Guardian Angel.''

"Children have especially beautiful Guardian Angels. Their garments are light-blue decorated with pearls, with a beautiful ever-lasting crown of roses around their heads."

"We understood that no matter how small a particle falls, the Angels are ever-ready to collect it and bring it back to the ciborium."

sang in order to carry out this special duty: "And suddenly with the Angel there was a great throng of the heavenly host, praising God and singing: 'Glory to God in the highest heaven, and peace to men who enjoy his favour.'" (Lk 2:13-14) Let us bring Padre Pio into this little story by recounting an incident which occurred during his life-time and which involves the Angels singing once again:

On one occasion in the Friary of Our Lady of Grace, a number of friars heard some heavenly music; voices singing in beautiful harmony, but they couldn't explain where it came from. At that hour during the day, nobody sang in the church, so they went to Padre Pio to see if he could give them an answer. He was absorbed in prayer at that time and, jumping at the sound of their voices, he replied: "Why are you all so surprised? They are the voices of Angels who are taking souls from Purgatory into Paradise." Naturally, the friars were speechless, but their hearts were filled with joy as they pondered on the wonderful experience which they had had.

On another occasion, two young spiritual children of Padre Pio were sitting on the beach on a Summer's afternoon; it was precisely the month of August. Suddenly, they heard unexplainable voices coming from the direction of the Gargano mountain, and as they listened, these voices became, little by little, more clear. They described the voices as being, not earthly, but heavenly; a beautiful choir, the like of which they had never heard before. This music lifted their souls and transported them to the heights. The voices were praising Our Blessed Lady and were, in fact, singing the Litany of the Holy Rosary. Gradually the heavenly music began to fade away until it could no longer be heard at all.

The two young men were dumbfounded; they simply couldn't understand what had happened, but it all became very clear to them when they went to visit Padre Pio. They asked him what the singing could have been, and he replied: "Silly boys, you didn't understand? It was the Angels who were praising Our Lady, from above the

Friary. Thank the Lord for the special grace which you received!"

We already know that Padre Pio, from the time he was a very young boy, was on very good terms with his Guardian Angel but I would like to relate another little story from his early years, which emphasizes the fact that angelic presences were quite usual to him:

Padre Pio was baptized in the church of Our Lady of the Angels, now the church of Saint Anne, and here, he often celebrated Mass and prayed to Our Lady of Liberty, Patroness of the town. The parish priest, Salvatore Pannullo, was very fond of Padre Pio, even when he was only a simple altar-boy and before he became a student for the priesthood. So much so, that the other young boys used to become quite jealous which, in turn, made Padre Pio very sympathetic towards them. "We all knew", said one of these young men, "that Francesco (Padre Pio) was a very ill young man, and as we knew that he took the franciscan rules very seriously, we used to make fun of him.

"One day, as we were walking together", continued the same young man, "the parish priest, Salvatore Pannullo, listened more to Francesco's conversation than to that of the rest of us. So much so, that at one point, he told us all to stay quiet and listen to what Francesco said that he had heard. He had heard a choir of Angels singing, and bells ringing from not so very far away from us, and he indicated to us the direction from which the sound came; it was a deserted area of the road. None of the rest of us heard anything, and the silence was broken with our peals of laughter."

A group of young people; full of fun and high spirits, laughing at Padre Pio's story of the Angels singing. We really cannot blame them as I'm sure if I were in the same position, I would be a little bit doubtful too. However, knowing what I now do about our beloved Father, I can only conclude once again that indeed, "An Angel Sang".

THE BUSY ANGELS

"... Angels came and ministered to him." (Mt 4:11)

It would appear from the writings of Padre Pio, and from the stories of those who were lucky enough to have met and spoken to him, that the Angels are not creatures who stand idly by our sides, on the contrary, from the evidence available, it appears that they are prepared to travel any distance to obey the simplest of our commands. And, in between orders from their individual charges, they guide, protect and enlighten when the need arises. This chapter is really a conglomeration of incidents related to me by various people or gathered together from various sources:

"I was praying to my Guardian Angel", writes Padre Lino Barbato, "and I sent him to Padre Pio asking him to intercede to the Lord to obtain a favour for a lady who was very ill but things did not change at all for her. When I met Padre Pio I said: 'Padre, I prayed to my Guardian Angel to help this lady; is it possible that he did not do his job?' He replied: 'What do you believe, that he is disobedient like you and me?' "

* * *

The following story was related by Father Eusebio, who was very close to Padre Pio: Apparently, he was travelling to London by plane, against Padre Pio's advice, as he did not want him to use that mode of transport. Whilst the plane was crossing "La Manica", a violent storm put it in danger. In the general terror, Fr. Eusebio recited an act of contrition and, not knowing what else to do, he sent his Guardian Angel to Padre Pio asking to be released from danger.

On his return to San Giovanni, Fr.

Eusebio went to Padre Pio who greeted him warmly saying: "Young man, how are you? Did everything go well?" "Padre", replied Fr. Eusebio, "I feared for my life." "Then why didn't you obey?", said Padre Pio. Immediately, Father Eusebio told him that he had sent his Guardian Angel to which the Padre replied smilingly: "Just as well he arrived on time!"

Father Eusebio also spent some time in Ireland where there is immense devotion to Padre Pio, and whilst there, many people came to ask his prayers so he always wrote to the friars in San Giovanni Rotondo asking them to convey the many requests to Padre Pio. After a while, he became a little afraid of making a nuisance of himself, so he decided to send his Guardian Angel to talk with Padre Pio's. "Only God knows", he said, "how many times I used this means which, all in all, seemed to go very well."

When he returned to San Giovanni, he went to say hello to Padre Pio and asked him: "Padre, did they do their work, my Angel and yours, did mine come wher sent him?" He replied quickly: "If he had to come every time you sent him, he was not left idle!"

* * *

Writing for his book "Padre Pio da Pietrelcina", Alessandro da Ripabottoni says: "One morning, I was a little late and, afraid that I would not be in time for Padre Pio's Mass, I said: 'My Guardian Angel, go to Padre Pio and tell him to wait a little before celebrating; as a sign that you will do me this favour, lift off his skull-cap!' I hurried to the Friary and, arriving at the church, I saw Padre Pio in front of the altar steps, ready to begin the Mass. I attended the Mass, after which I went into the Sacristy and saw that Padre Pio was opening the cupboards in search of something. I said to him: 'Padre, what are you looking for?' He replied: 'My son, I can't find my skull-cap anymore! I remembered then what I had said to my Guardian Angel so I told Padre Pio. He looked at me in a manner which said, 'Now you believe it?' He started to look for the skull-cap again and finally, he found it in his hood."

* * *

Most of us, at one time or another during our lives, have shed tears, perhaps because of the death of a loved one, a hurt inflicted upon us by someone whom we considered a friend or simply because of the sheer desire to relieve ourselves of something that had built up in us over a period of time. Quite often, we look on our tears as being utterly useless, perhaps telling ourselves to "buck up and do something to rectify the situation". Tears, however, are not such useless things as we discover from Padre Pio's own words on the subject, when he said to someone who had been crying a lot: "Your tears were collected by the Angels and were placed in a gold chalice and you will find them when you present yourself before God."

* * *

The following story was related to me by a friend from the U.S.A.: "My mother died in 1947 and I was feeling very depressed. A few months later, after retiring one evening, I recalled a story that I had read or heard; that if you wished to receive help from Padre Pio you should pray to your Guardian Angel to contact Padre Pio's to obtain the favour from him. With not a little scepticism, I said the prayer. It was, I believe, that night that I awakened to see, in my dark room, an elderly man with a beard standing at my bed-side looking down at me. His face was beautiful, the expression so kind and peaceful that I had no fear. How long the vision lasted, I don't remember; it could have been a second or minutes, but it was so vivid that I got up from my bed, put the light on and looked around the room. It appeared that the figure was that of Padre Pio, but I will leave that for you to judge." Perhaps Padre Pio came in answer to her Guardian Angel's request for help.

* * *

"Father, permit me to tell you a little story", wrote a friend of mine. "Two or three months ago, a young woman at our place of work sent one of the scapulars (which you blessed for me with Padre Pio's glove) to her brother who was to undergo serious surgery; they were much afraid of cancer. This man did not know of Padre Pio at that time, but he did wear the scapular. The operation was a success; no cancer, thank God, and he is already back at work. His hours are long and he works until very late at night.

"One night, he was on his way home and, at about 11 P.M., his car broke down; he was many miles away from home on a dark road. He tried to hitch-hike for a couple of hours but nobody stopped for him; I imagine he must have been very concerned. He began to pray to Padre Pio and became so immersed in prayer that he did not notice a truck pull up in front of him. The driver got out, asked what was wrong and took a look at his car; it was beyond repair. Even though they were travelling in opposite directions, and the man lived many miles away, the truck driver insisted that he would take him home right to his front door and... refused to be paid!

"This story put me in mind of Padre Pio sending his Angel to someone in need. Could it have been that way? God bless Padre Pio for the wonders he still continues to perform."

* * *

"Dear Father Alessio", wrote Nick Cocucci, U.S.A. "We have just recovered from a massive snow storm here. This week, I slipped on the ice and I fell twice. Today, I thought I was going to break my back but I came away with only a cut left elbow; truly my Guardian Angel must have been with me. When I receive Holy Communion this coming Sunday, I am going to receive it for my Guardian Angel".

* * *

And another letter: "Father, my little

daughter was born perfect but at five weeks old, she caught a cold. I took her to the doctor and he gave her some medicines and in a few days she was almost better again. Then she caught pneumonia and had to be taken into hospital. She then started to lose body fluid and the doctor told my husband and I that there was no hope of her living as she was not responding to treatment. I stood beside the incubator in which she had been placed; she was being fed through her head and her tongue was all swollen.

"I wanted to hold her but I could not touch her through the glass. My husband's grandmother was there and I said to her that I thought my baby would die. She said: 'Ask Padre Pio to make her better; send him your Guardian Angel.' I put my arms around the incubator and I said: 'I send my Guardian Angel to you, Padre Pio, to make my baby live', and at that moment she shivered as if something had touched her.

"The next morning, I rang the hospital and there was no change in her condition. All that day, I kept saying these words to

Padre Pio: 'I send my Guardian Angel to you to make my baby live.' At six o'clock that evening, I rang the hospital again and the doctor told me that she had improved a little, I knew then that Padre Pio had accepted my Guardian Angel and had heard my prayers. My little daughter came home from hospital four weeks later, fully recovered."

* * *

"Dear Father Alessio", wrote Mrs. Judith Ng, "have you started to write 'SEND ME YOUR GUARDIAN ANGEL' yet? I hope you don't mind, but I have named my Angel after you! I call him Alessio and he takes very good care of me... As regards having called my Guardian Angel after you, I don't know how he feels about it either as he doesn't speak with me! However, I'm sure he considers it an honour..."

* * *

"Thank you, Father Alessio, for sending me 'The Voice of Padre Pio' ", wrote Josephine O'Hara. "I love reading it and the article on Padre Pio's Guardian Angel was most beautiful; I have read it several times. I will encourage the small children I teach to have devotion to the Guardian Angel..."

* * *

"During a recent trip from California to New Mexico", wrote Mrs. B. Valdez, "we had car trouble just six miles outside of Winslow, Arizona. Our car heated up to the highest point on the gauge, and we stopped on the shoulder of the road. My husband tried waving cars down but, after half an hour, nobody stopped to help us and there was a lot of traffic on the highway. That was when I decided to pray; I asked my Guardian Angel to ask Padre Pio to come and help. I had barely started praying when someone stopped to give us 'Prestone'. We continued on our trip, then our car over heated again and the

'Prestone' boiled over. Nobody would stop to help this time, either. I asked Padre Pio for help again and somebody with 'Prestone' stopped once more. We once again continued on our journey and the same thing happened again! By that time, my husband decided that we needed someone to tow us into town. I had barely started Padre Pio's favourite novena prayer when a sheriff drove up and gave my husband a lift into town to get a tow-truck. Wc were towed into town, where we got the car fixed properly. Thanks to my Guardian Angel for fetching Padre Pio! And thanks to Padre Pio for sending us some help.

"We were already well on our way out of town to California when I rememberd that I had forgotten something so we drove back to the house. As an after-thought, I saw my Padre Pio novena on the headboard of the bed and put it in my purse. Isn't it amazing?"

* * *

"All the houses around me have been broken into", wrote Mrs. A. Fontana, "but mine has never been, because every time I leave the house, I leave my Guardian Angel to look after it!"

* * *

The following letter was sent to me by Miss T. Doyle, U.S.A.: "On January 14th., a patient, of whom I was quite fond, died at about 4.P.M. I was in the dining room for dinner at about 5 P.M. and I saw him being taken out. I closed my eyes, not wanting to look and then I decided to pray. Three times I said: 'Eternal rest grant unto his soul, oh Lord...' Suddenly, I felt a quite pronounced tapping on my back, immediately below my right shoulder-blade. Three times I felt this as I was saying the prayer. The second time, I quickly turned my head but there was nobody there. I continued my prayers, wondering. Finishing them for my friend's soul, I opened my eyes again and I looked at his still, covered form. I then told another patient's wife who was at a nearby table, what had happened, and I forget exactly what she said but it was something like the following: 'Maybe his Guardian Angel is asking you to pray for him?' When this happened, I noticed the aroma of gardenias. I turned my head to the left and the aroma was not there..."

* * *

Devotion to Padre Pio in Ireland particulary strong and consequently, many graces are received through Padre Pio's intercession; perhaps with the Angels' help sometimes. The following incident occurred in the village of Lusk, Co. Dublin and was related to me by Miss Joan Thornton who is presently working for Padre Pio in San Giovanni Rotondo.

And old lady was making her way to Mass, as she did every day of her life. However, this morning was particulary dark, so she was wondering how she would cross the bridge which lead to the church. Instinctively she said: "Oh Lord, light my way". Suddenly, the whole place was lit up, so much so, that her pathway across the bridge became completely visible! She then found no difficulty whatsoever in making her way over it. No sooner had she reached the other side of the bridge when the bright light disappeared. Could this have been her Guardian Angel? After all, remember the prayer: "... to light and guard, to rule and guide."

* * *

Padre Mariano spent many years at Padre Pio's side and, of course, noticed his particular devotion to the Guardian Angel. Let us hear what he has to say in this regard: "Especially when he administered the sacrament of penance, he used to advise the penitents to venerate the Angels", said Padre Mariano. "He used to recommend that they always act in the presence of God and the Guardian Angel. It is well known to all, that Padre Pio used to receive our Guardian Angels who brought him all our requests and messages. I personally sent him mine many times, when I was far away from San Giovanni Rotondo, and he used to assure me that he got the message or requests for graces and help, through the Guardian Angel. Each time when I asked him if my Angel had done his job, he would answer me: 'What do you think, that the Angels are disobedient like you and I?' I remember very well, one time when I was in Lourdes and I sent Padre Pio my Guardian Angel, to greet him with a message and a request for a grace, and when I had done this, I smelled the characteristic perfume associated with Padre Pio. When I returned to the Friary in San Giovanni, I asked him to explain to me the meaning of the perfume, which I had smelled from so very far away. He answered me: 'As regards the perfume, I love you, and as regards the Guardian Angel, yes, I received his message; he arrived safely. Do you think he is disobedient like you and I?' "

Padre Mariano continued: "Padre Pio had also a great devotion to Saint Michael the Archangel. A remarkable soul saw, whilst in the U.S.A., a vision: Padre Pio appeared to be in an infant's cradle, and the protective wings of Saint Michael formed an arch over it. This person was not able to approach Padre Pio so, I eventually asked him what the vision meant and he said: 'Padre Mariano, it is true. Woe to me if Saint Michael had not protected me. At this hour, I would already be under the feet of the devil.' "

Padre Mariano concluded: "May the Lord be thanked and blessed, for giving to the Church, in this century, the Servant of God, Padre Pio of Pietrelcina."

* * *

These little snippets were not substantial enough to form full stories in their own right, but I thought they were too beautiful to leave out altogether, so I hope the readers have enjoyed them.

"TWENTY FOUR - TWENTY FIVE"

"If there be for him an angel, a mediator, one of the thousand, to declare to man what is right for him."
(Mt 33:23)

Sometime before Padre Pio went to his eternal reward, two friends of ours went to San Giovanni Rotondo to confess to him. They were both sitting in one of the pews of the little church waiting for their turn, and Padre Pellegrino had assigned to them the numbers 24 and 25 on the register of that day. One of the two was praying fervently with the rosary in her hands and was very recollected. The other, on the contrary, was feeling rather uncomfortable because she was tempted to defer, until the following day, her confession, so that she could stay another day near Padre Pio.

She told her friend that she intended to postpone her confession until the following day but was given a questioning look. However, she insisted, so, leaving the bench, she told Padre Pellegrino of her decision and he said: "If you like, you can go to confession tomorrow, but be sure to leave the church before your turn arrives."

Feeling very happy, she went back to the bench to tell her friend, thinking that she would follow, but she did not move. As she was so much against it, the decision was made to remain in the church. It was then she thought of her Guardian Angel so she prayed to him fervently, with a strong faith, hoping that he would help her. She told him to go to Padre Pio and ask him not to hear her confession that morning. "You see", she said to him with human feeling, "Padre Pio is there; you don't have to walk a long distance. I beg you, go to him!"

Padre Pio could not have known anything as he was immersed in his ministry of the confessional. However, Padre Pellegrino, in a loud voice, seemed to pronounce the numbers of the penitents very quickly. There was a competition between the beating of her heart and the numbers being called. "Eighteen, nineteen, twenty, twenty-one", said Padre Pellegrino. When she heard him say: "Twenty-two, twenty-three", she realized that there were only about five minutes left before her turn came. Angrily, she addressed her Guardian Angel and exploded: "Go, go", she said to him. "Whatever they say about you, I don't believe a word of it; it's just not true." Then, "Twenty-four, twenty-five". She was about to answer to confirm her presence but suddenly, Padre Pio abruptly got up and came out of the confessional. Looking at Padre Pellegrino, he shouted: "Eh, basta", "that's enough, I'm tired. Do you want to kill me today?" And, with that, he turned towards the main altar.

Padre Pellegrino was very surprised, but you could have knocked our friend down with a feather. However, she kept on her feet and did not faint because, evidently, her Guardian Angel was close at her side once again, holding her steady!

MARY THE AMERICAN

"... Where have you come from...?"
(Gen 16:8)

It would be difficult to write a book concerning Padre Pio without some mention of a saintly lady who spent most of her life near his side. Mary Pyle was born in Morristown, New Jersey, daughter of James Tolman Pyle and Adeline McAlpin. Her family was quite wealthy, her father having made a fortune in the soap business. All her family were faithful Presbyterians and Mary grew up in that atmsphere. In her infancy and adolescence, she differed greatly from her four brothers and one sister in intelligence and piety. Her education was mainly obtained in private schools and it was privately also, that she learned to speak fluently, Spanish, Italian, French and German. She also studied music, singing and dance to her advantage. Her youth was spent frequenting the high society together with her family. She enjoyed horse riding very much and, on one occasion, after a severe fall, which resulted in a foot complaint later in life she was heard to say: "This is in reparation for all the dancing I've done."

During her adolescent years, Mary was taken to Europe quite often and, on one of these occasions, she met the famous doctor Maria Montessori, propagator of a revolutionary new method of teaching from infancy, with particular regard to the retarded child. This resulted in Maria Montessori asking Mary if she would like to travel with her and act as her interpreter. At that time, Mary could speak English, Spanish, Italian and German fluently. During her travels, she became profoundly interested in the Catholic faith and, at the age of 25 years, she was baptized in the catholic church in Spain. Her mother, on hearing the news, was horrified and in Mary's own words: "When she was making her will, she excluded me as if I were not her daughter."

At the age of 35, Mary, having heard about Padre Pio, decided to go and see him for herself. We do not know much about that first meeting except that Mary herself said: "We looked at one another only. Then, I fell on my knees and said: 'Padre'. He put his wounded hands on my head and said to me: 'My daughter, do not travel anymore. Stay here.'" Thus Mary built herself a villa close to the Friary; furnished it in a franciscan manner and settled down under the spiritual direction of Padre Pio.

Mary naturally began to receive english-speaking visitors in her home and thus a lively correspondence between the spiritual children of Padre Pio commenced. In many of her letters, the Guardian Angels were mentioned and, for her, as for Padre Pio, they were of the utmost importance: "Dear Catherine Morran", she wrote on 2 February 1958,

"Just a few lines written in great haste, to thank you from the bottom of my heart for your letter, and also for the Christmas card and offering. I gave it all for the new church which is really progressing beautifully. I knew you would not mind as it gave me greater pleasure than if I had bought something for myself. When the church is finished, I do hope that you will be able to come and see it. I warn you that I am very old. Do not forget to send your Guardian Angel to our beloved Padre Pio and he will hear you. Lots of love and a very special blessing from Padre Pio.

Your far away sister
Mary Pyle

And on another occasion she wrote:

"Dear Mrs. Julia Rogers,

I have received your letter, good wishes and pretty card and have recommended you spiritually to Padre Pio, as you can do yourself. He sends you his blessing and will do so every time you ask it through your Guardian Angel."

Mary Pyle

Mary always asked those who wrote to her to pray to the Guardian Angel and surely, this was not without encouragement from Padre Pio himself. She was one of the few women with whom he would stop for a while to have a chat. Not only was she close to our beloved Padre, but she also took care of his parents in her villa when old-age came upon them. They both, in fact, died in her home. The following little story concerning the Guardian Angels was taken from the book * "Maria Pyle" by Bonaventura Massa:

"In the early months of 1946, Zi' Orazio, as everybody called Padre Pio's father, fell down the stairs in Mary's house. He was really very lucky that he was not killed with the fall. When he complained to Padre Pio of some of the pain he suffered afterwards, Padre Pio said to him: 'Instead, thank your Guardian Angel who placed a cushion on every step!"

---

* - In Italian only.

Such was a brief look at the life of Mary Pyle who, without a doubt, left her mark on San Giovanni Rotondo. She died in franciscan poverty, leaving her house to the Friary but she has certainly not been forgotten here, in this little village on the Gargano Mountain.

"They are the constant companions of our journeys and the mute witnesses of our everyday lives."

"One day, while Padre Pio was passing through the Saint Francis room, he was approached by a young man who asked him if he could become his spiritual child."

"... I am always close to you, my beloved young man."

"Father Alessio is good-hearted, and is like a little faithful puppy-dog."

Padre Pio

THE MECHANICALLY - MINDED ANGEL

"... Then Manoah knew that he was the angel of the Lord."
(Judg 15:21)

From what we have previously read, we know that the Angels are quite capable of getting behind the wheel of a car, but it would appear, from the following story, that they can also lift up and rectify faults in these "machines" when they are called upon to do so. One of Padre Pio's spiritual children told the following story:

In the year 1959, both she and her husband were returning from a trip to Passo Scuro, near Rome. They had never been to that place before even though they had passed it many times. Whilst on their way, her husband, who was driving, became distracted and failed to notice a deposit of stones which had accumulated on the right-hand side of the road. This heap of stones was higher than one metre and about one-and-a-half metres in width.

She always turned to her Guardian Angel in times of need and especially when she was travelling by car, because Padre Pio has told her to do this. So, when she saw the danger, she turned immediately to the faithful Angel and suddenly, the car lifted off the ground and jumped over the obstacle, landing very gently on the other side. To make a long story short, the car flew, and within a short time they were back home safe and sound.

The same person told another story: On another occasion, she and her husband were going to San Severo, where they had a beautiful villa by the sea. Apart from the Summer months, they spent nearly every Sunday there; leaving on Saturday evening and returning to Rome on Monday morning. One Saturday, they left for the villa with their fairly large French poodle. They had intended to spend some days at

San Severo, to prepare the house for the Summer months. Ten or twelve kilometres before they should turn off for San Severo, the car broke down. They pushed it to the side of the road to wait for someone who might give them some assistance, but nobody did. Cars sped by, one after the other without stopping.

They were there two hours and didn't know what to do; night was beginning to fall. Eventually, she suggested to her husband that they pray to Padre Pio (he was still alive at that time), so that he might send an Angel to help them. Her husband, a little doubtful, answered: "Go ahead and try!" And with that, they began to wait patiently.

After about ten minutes, they saw a black car coming towards them. It stopped near their car, and a beautiful young man of noble countenance, very elegantly dressed in blue, stepped out. Coming towards them, he said: "Well, what happened?" Her husband, in a few words, explained the situation. The young man immediately answered: "I'll take care of it now. You'll see that we will fix everything." And he lifted the bonnet to see the engine. Her husband, who knew about cars, had already done this, and at that time, he had been driving for fourty years.

The young man then looked at her husband and said: "Look, you lost all the water from the radiator, and it's burnt out. Take the can and fill it up with water. Near here, there is a farm-house, which has a well; take the water from there." Her husband, like an automaton, took the little can, which was empty, from the boot, and he went to the place which the young man had indicated. He crossed over the Via Aurelia, with ease, although it is generally impossible to walk there because of the heavy traffic.

In the meantime, the young man took from his car, a black box, from which he produced a role of adhesive tape, and started to seal the radiator. She remembered her amazement at seeing his beautiful hands; the fingers tapered and agile. She noticed also, that the dog, which was well used to guarding the car, and which barked every time a stranger approached, was very calm and looked at him contentedly.

Her husband brought back the water; the young man refilled the radiator, closed the bonnet and said: "Now you can return home safely, anyhow, you are quite near. But tomorrow, bring the car to be checked immediately." They thanked him from the bottom of their hearts and he, smilingly said: "Ciao... Ciao..." (" 'Bye... Bye...").

As they set off, her husband turned on the headlights; she wanted to see the licence plate of the young man's car, but, to her amazement, she discovered that there was none! In it's place was a long white strip with hieroglyphical writing on it. There was neither the name of the city, nor numbers! She could see everything very well, as the young man's car was directly in front of them, and was going very slowly, whilst the headlights illuminated everything. Before they turned off for San Severo, they stopped to say goodbye to him, and he waved his hand out of the car in response. Then, unexpectecly, he disappeared. Even though they should have seen the car, as that area of the Via Aurelia was completely straight.

They reached home in a dreamy state, and started to reflect on what had happened. They asked themselves how that young man came directly to them; how he knew that they had an empty can in the boot, and that they had only a short distance to go before they reached home. They had not told him their destination. And the dog, contrary to it's normal way of behaving, remained very calm and did not bark at all. They wondered why the young man's car did not have a licence plate, and for all this, they remained amazed and dumbfounded. Ever since, when they passed that area again, they tried to find the little farm-house and the well, but despite their diligent efforts, they never succeeded!

"In faith", the lady concerned was heard to say, "I can say that Padre Pio confirmed that it was an Angel who came to our aid, but, above all, it was he who helped us as we had asked him to send us an Angel to give us assistance."

Really, the whole incident seems rather incredible. But that is the true story and, no matter how one looks at it, it was more than a little unusual to say the least. Lest the reader should decide, having discovered all this, to doze at the wheel of his car, or to deliberately have it break down, in order to see if he receives the same help, I would strongly advise against it. Not that I don't believe that the required help would come, but we must leave the Angels time to do some other work, such as waking people up; singing hymns; translating other languages; fighting the devil; travelling around the world; delivering letters..... Well done, "little boy".

VISIBLE COMPANION

"Do not neglect to show hospitality to strangers, for thereby some have entertained angels unawares."
(Heb 13:2)

During World War I, Padre Pio served as a soldier in the Italian army. He began this service in Naples, and the year was 1917, two years after he had first presented himself. Bundled up in a uniform too large for him, and occupied sometimes as orderly, sometimes as porter or dustman, Padre Pio, for all his good intentions, found the going difficult, and consequently, on many occasions he became so ill that he had to be sent home on sick-leave. On one of these occasions, when he was returning to Pietrelcina, something extraordinary happened, and this incident was told by the good Padre himself:

Having travelled to Benevento by train, he found that he did not have enough money to pay for his bus ticket to Pietrelcina. The ticket cost a little less than two lire, and he had only a quarter of the amount. Not without some hesitation, and feeling very anxious, he got on the bus, whilst at the same time, putting his trust in Divine Providence. He took a scat at the back, where he could confess his difficulty to the conductor without the embarrassment of the other passengers' hearing him. Then, he saw an unusual character getting on board; fashionably dressed and with a very new piece of luggage. He took a seat right beside Padre Pio and, resting the luggage on his knees, he opened it. Then, taking out a thermos flask, he poured some of it's contents - hot coffee - into a glass and offered it to the young soldier. Padre Pio at first refused it, even though he was feverish, and trembling with cold in his clumsy clothes, but his companion, insistent as he was, obliged him to accept it.

The steaming hot cup of coffee was more than welcome, but all the while, Padre Pio's eyes were on the conductor who was mercilessly approaching, examining the other passengers' tickets. The poor soldier multiplied his supplications to the Lord. He was preparing himself to say to the conductor that he would pay for his ticket as soon as he reached his destination, but he wasn't given a chance to say anything at all. Turning suddenly to him, the conductor said: "Soldier, your ticket has already been paid for".

The soldier (Padre Pio), absolutely astounded by this, turned suspicious eyes on his companion and wondered who had paid for his ticket. He wanted to ask the conductor, but didn't dare. Eventually, they arrived at Pietrelcina, and as soon as he had stepped out of the bus, Padre Pio turned to thank his companion for the last time, and to say goodbye to him. But, although he looked everywhere, he was not to be found; he had disappeared!

When Padre Pio had finished telling this story, he did not make any suggestions as to the identity of his travelling companion; evidently out of holy humility, but for us, it was very easy to guess who the "culprit" was: his invisible companion who, for a time, became visible.

ANGELS IN THE SKY

"And David lifted his eyes and saw the angel of the lord standing between earth and heaven..."
(Chron 21:16)

There is a beautiful story about Padre Pio and the Angels which occurred around the time of his death. This was related to me by a Mr. J. Kelly from the U.S.A. and the story goes as follows: In September, 1968, he left the States for San Giovanni Rotondo; he attended Padre Pio's Mass and spent the first few days in recollected prayer. On one of these days, Padre Pio did not say Mass in public due to illness, but on the 22nd. he did, in the presence of many people. It was the 50th. anniversary of his receiving the stigmata. During the celebration, Padre Pio did not appear to be so well, so afterwards, Mr. Kelly left the church feeling more than a little troubled.

The following morning, he got up at about 3 o'clock, to be in time for Padre Pio's Mass at five. The crowd waited patiently outside the church for three hours and finally, one of the friars came to say that Padre Pio had passed away. Before dawn, Mr. Kelly had seen Angels in the sky so he ran over to his friend who was with him, to point them out, and he saw them clearly too. One big one over the hospital and one over the church, with little ones all around. When day-light came, they all disappeared.

It seemed that the Angels who served Padre Pio devotedly during his life-time, were around to bring him safely into the next world.

ANGEL OF THE SICK

"...And He healed them all..."
(Mt 12:15)

Millions of people had made their way to visit Padre Pio during his life time, and he welcomed each one in turn with open arms, but in a particular way, he welcomed our sick brothers and sisters and treated them with great compassion. In each one of them, he saw the suffering Jesus, and accordingly, his charity towards them knew no bounds. In these few pages, I would like to relate to you, some incidents concerning our beloved Padre and the sick, and of course, the Angels come into the picture once again:

A soul very close to Padre Pio had a

sister who was very ill with pneumonia, and this was in the days when the condition was not so curable as it is today. The lady concerned went to the Friary, but, when she reached it she found it closed and consequently, fell into a state of desperation. However, thinking of her Guardian Angel, she said: "Padre Pio, help me! My Guardian Angel, go and tell Padre Pio that I have come for his help, otherwise my sister will die." At that moment, from the window of the church, she heard Padre Pio's voice, and he said: "Who is calling me at this hour? What's wrong?" This poor soul told of the pitiful state of her sister and Padre Pio, whose heart was always bursting with love for his fellow men, went in bilocation to the invalid, and she recovered!

There is also a story concerning a young lady who, having been told by the doctors that her husband could die from one minute to the next, following a heart-attack, sent her Guardian Angel to Padre Pio, so that he might pray for her husband. One night, shortly after, she dreamt of the beautifully radiant stigmatized priest. She immediately asked him to bless her husband, and Padre Pio replied that he would, so he placed his hands on the man's head, and then disappeared. The following morning, the man had recovered and was feeling very well. The doctors were amazed and, of course, his family was overjoyed.

The following testimony, which could also be the work of the Guardian Angel, was given by 'His Excellency, Alfredo Viola, Bishop of Salto, Uruguay:

"In the year 1937, Mgr. Ferdinando Damiani, on the discovery that he had a heart condition, came to San Giovanni Rotondo with the idea of dying near Padre Pio, and of being assisted by him.

"In fact, when he was in the Friary, he suffered a very bad heart-attack which, for two hours, held his life in danger. Padre Pio was sent for, and, as at that time he was in the confessional, he did not come until the danger had passed. When later the Mgr. complained that he did not come sooner, Padre Pio smilingly said: 'I knew that you would not die; that's why I continued to confess the people.'

"When Mgr. Damiani later improved, Padre Pio told him to go back to Uruguay, and to continue his work (at that time, he was Vicar General to Mgr. Camacho, Bishop of Salto whose assistant I was), because when he would reach the point of death, Padre Pio himself would come to assist him. So, he continued with his Office, and his ailment gradually worsened.

"In September 1941, Bishop Camacho had already died, and as I was the Bishop of the Diocese, I held a vocational congress on the occasion of the 25th anniversary of my ordination to the priesthood. It was also the 50th. anniversary of my predecessor, who had died in May, 1940. During this meeting, the first stone of the Minor Seminary was laid.

"The congress began with great solemnity and the Papal Nuncio, Mgr. Alberto Levame, was present, along with the Archbishop of Montevideo, Mgr. Antonio Maria Barbieri, and the Bishop of

Florida, Mgr. Michele Paternain; all were guests in the Archbishop's house. After the first day, precisely during the night of the 11th. and 12th. of September, Mgr. Damiani suffered an attack of "angina pectoris"; it was after mid-night.

"Mgr. Barbieri, who was in Mgr. Damiani's house up until 11 o'clock that night; and even after, had gone fast asleep, when suddenly, he was awakened by a banging on the door of his room. He opened the door and heard a voice saying: 'Go and assist Mgr. Damiani as he's dying.' Mgr. Barbieri said, that in the shadow, he thought he saw the outline of a Capuchin friar.

"The knocking on the door had been heard by a priest, Rev. Fr. Francesco Navarro, who had been praying in the oratory of the Bishop's house.

"Mgr. Barbieri ran to Mgr. Damiani's room, finding all the doors without keys, but closed. Mgr. Damiani was in bed, with a little table, generally used by the sick, over it, and he was dying. Spread out on the table (we saw later), were the pills called "trinitrina", which evidently he had tried to take, but couldn't reach them, and a rough copy of a telegram, written by a shaky hand, which said:

'Padre Pio, San Giovanni Rotondo. The heart spasms are continuing; they are killing me - Damiano.' "

This telegram had never been sent. The poor soul, all alone in the face of death, tried to reach his tablets so that he could revive himself and ask somebody to send it to Padre Pio. Thus, his beloved friend would know just how ill he was. But God has many ways of assisting his faithful servants. Divine Providence always sends help to those in need. Did the good Lord enlighten Padre Pio as to his friend's condition? Did He send Padre Pio in bilocation or did Mgr. Damiani send his Guardian Angel to our beloved Padre? Let us continue with Mgr. Alfredo Viola's testimony:

"Fully aware, the Mgr. asked Mgr. Barbieri to give him extreme-unction. The Archbishop woke me up immediately; I woke up the Nuncio and Mgr. Paternain, and the other priests who were sleeping in the house. Mgr. Damiani confessed to Father Navarro; he received extreme unction from the parish priest of the cathedral and was visited by his doctor, who said that nothing could be done for him. He died half-an-hour later, assisted by four Bishops and six priests.

"That was the manner in which he died; well attended, in the early hours of 12 September 1941. I must say, that given the circumstances of the congress, his funeral was most solemn and was attended by four Bishops and more than fifty priests. This was, for us, an extraordinarily large number, and the whole occasion was more like a triumphant procession than a funeral cortège; the number of mourners was immense.

"In faith, I sign and seal this declaration, at San Giovanni Rotondo, on the 26 November, 1958."

Seal
Alfridi Episcopi
Saltenis - Uruguay

†Alfredo Viola
Bishop of Salto

Let us now take a closer look at the facts: Padre Pio had promised the Mgr. that he would be with him at his hour of death; Mgr. Barbieri saw a shadowy outline of a Capuchin friar in the corridor; the telegram was never sent to Padre Pio, and yet nobody could have been better assisted at the hour of death. Evidently, Padre Pio had a hand in this, but how did he know about the situation? Was our little friend, the Angel, at work once again? We don't know, but, aware as we are of the extraordinary activities of these celestial creatures, one could be excused for suspecting that the Guardian Angel was on duty once again.

Quite a number of years have passed since Padre Pio departed from this earth. His absence was a shock to the world, but much more to the town of San Giovanni Rotondo. When the thousands of people present at his funeral made their way home, in every corner of every street, the only words to be heard were: "All is finished. Who will come again to this far isolated mountain?" The fear of the townspeople was reinforced by the departure of the residential people who had settled down near Our Lady of Grace Friary. All was a false alarm. Padre Pio's spirituality, which embraced 52 years of prayer and suffering, had taken root in the hard unyielding rock of the Gargano mountain. The seed of spirituality which he had sown in the hearts of all his spiritual children could not be without fruit. Padre Pio had worked devotedly for our sick brothers and sisters during his life time and this work would continue on even after his death.

After their first sense of bewilderment because of the absence of their spiritual father, the friars embarked on the projects for the sick, which Padre Pio had spoken about many years before. His first and dearest project, the hospital, was already far advanced. The work however, was continued to the point of making it the most modern and well equipped hospital in southern Italy; more than fit to welcome the sick in that area. Then the friars' thoughts turned towards the handicapped and the elderly, all of whom were very dear to our beloved Padre's heart. After Padre Pio's advice, many handicapped children, abandoned by their parents, are now given love and attention in provisory buildings, waiting for the day when the new Centre for the handicapped will be completed. In order to avoid the difficult problem of bringing all those children to San Giovanni, the friars have opened up thirteen different Centres for the handicapped in the towns nearby.

The friars soon realized that, because of their physical difficulties, many of the sick were not able to visit Padre Pio's tomb. They decided, therefore, to follow in the footsteps of their spiritual father in his love for the sick, by building lifts, which would transport our incapacitated brothers and sisters to their much-desired goal, the tomb. Here, they could ask Padre Pio's prayers and intercession for their martyrized bodies.

These are the projects presently under construction, for the sick, on Padre Pio's mountain. Without a doubt, his love for these suffering souls was immense and, in this, he followed the example of our Lord, Jesus Christ, Who, being "moved with pity"* never failed to cure those who came to Him, while He was on this earth. Of course, Padre Pio was often helped in his work for the sick by the Angels, but under the circumstances, it would not be unreasonable to give him the title of "Angel of the Sick".

---

* - (Mk 1:41)

A SMILE

Smile
in his suffering
he has met life
smile
far from others
far from cement
far from dust
and dirt
in the emptiness
of a small space
hangs the hand
higher in the air without a sky
yet without movement in his feet
smile
destined to the chair
consecrated to rest
condemned to envy
in vain - heartily desiring
dreaming wishes
of dirty shoes - covered with mud
steep paths and green fields

falling down and scraped knees
long roads and weariness
he has legs of steel
a smile of a happy child
he has feet of wheels
and two eyes rich with light
pushed by others
nailed to his toy
he goes on smooth roads
with clean shoes
without calloused feet
gliding on life
like a paper boat
on the water of the sea
he goes unaware of the storm
in deep water
he goes bringing in light
his smile his suffering
to men drowning in water
that smile has been sufficient
to the world he has already made
it more beautiful
he has already given his life
his tribute of light - of good - of joy.

Silvestro Mischitelli

QUEEN OF ANGELS

"All honour to you Mary! Today you were raised above the choirs of angels to lasting glory with Christ." (From the Feast of the Assumption)

The very idea of writing on Padre Pio without mentioning his dear Mother, Our Blessed Lady, is quite out of the question. And, undoubtedly, the fact that the Angels helped Padre Pio a great deal in his priestly ministry, must be due, to a great extent, to the Madonna. He himself said: "Oh, Mary, sweetest Mother of priests, mediatrix and administratrix of all graces, I pray to you from the depths of my heart..." From these words, we can see, that even though the Angels carried out many orders given to them, to obtain many graces for people, they could not do this at all without the consent of the "Queen of Angels", who holds authority over them. Padre Pio also said: "Our Lady never refuses me a grace through the recitation of the Rosary." But the most important observation here, is that although these Angels worked so marvellously well for Padre Pio, they were under the authority of their "Queen", without whose permission they could do nothing at all.

It would be superfluous to say, that Padre Pio's filial devotion and love for Our Blessed Lady knew no bounds. He was never seen without Her Rosary in his hands, as he said: "Prayer is the key which opens up the heart of God", so it was through his prayer and his particular devotion to Our Blessed Mother that he received, for others, so many graces. In order to carry out these blessings, he was helped by the Angels.

In sum-total, behind all these marvellous gifts of Padre Pio, his extraordinary guidance of souls, his gift of bilocation and his camaraderie with the Angels, was Our Lady, who cherished him as a mother would a child, even to the point that, after he had been beaten by the devils one night in his room, She came and put a cushion under his head, in order to relieve his suffering somewhat. Let us now quote from the series of books: "City Of God" (The Coronation), and see just what Mary's position is amongst these celestial spirits. It begins with the visit of the Archangel Gabriel to her, informing her of her forthcoming departure from earthly life:

"The holy prince (Archangel Gabriel) descended with the rest to the Cenacle in Jerusalem and entered the oratory of the great Lady, where they found Her prostrate on the ground in the form of a cross, asking mercy for sinners. But, hearing the sound of their music and perceiving them present, She rose to her knees in order to hear the message and show respect for the ambassador of heaven and his companions, who in white and refulgent garments surrounded Her with wonderful delight and reverence. All of them had come with crowns and palms in their hands, each one with a different one; but all of them represented the diverse premiums and rewards of inestimable beauty and value to be conferred upon their great Queen and Lady. Gabriel saluted Her with the Ave Maria, and added thereto: 'Our Empress and Lady, the Omnipotent and the Holy of the holy sends us from his heavenly court to announce to Thee in his name the most happy end of thy pilgrimage and banishment upon earth in mortal life. Soon, O Lady, is that day and hour approaching, in which, according to thy longing desires, Thou shalt pass through natural death to the possession of the eternal and immortal life, which awaits Thee in glory and at the right hand of thy divine Son, our God. Exactly three years from today Thou shalt be taken up and received into the everlasting joy of the Lord, where all its inhabitants await Thee, longing for thy presence.'

"The most holy Mary heard this message with ineffable jubilee of her purest and most loving spirit, and, prostrating Herself again upon the earth,

"Thou shalt be the Lady and the Sovereign of the Seraphim, of all the ministering spirits, the Angels, and of the entire universe of creatures."

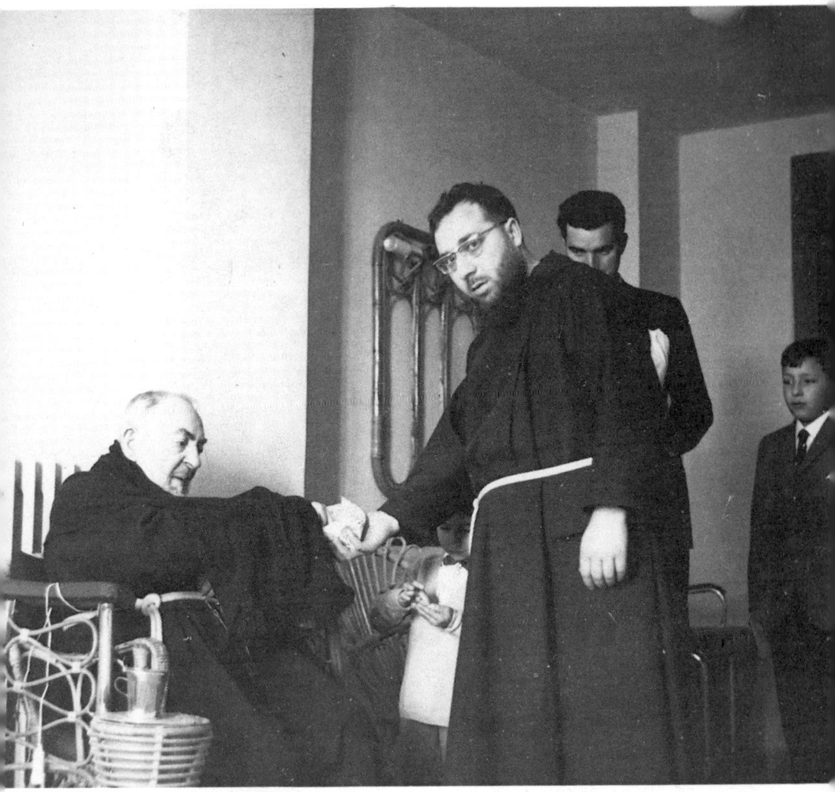

Doctors have said that Padre Pio did not eat enough to keep a four-year-old child alive, however, when offered a sweet, as he was in this case by Father Alessio, he accepted, more to please the offerer than to satisfy himself.

"Myriads of Angels continuously serve men throughout the course of their earthly lives."

In the latter years of his life, Padre Pio was not capable of moving about without the aid of his wheel-chair. His ever-present companion, Father Alessio, propells him along.

She answered in the same words as at the incarnation of the Word: 'Ecce ancilla Domini, fiat mihi secundum verbum tuum.' - 'Behold the handmaid of the Lord, be it done according to thy word.' Then She asked the holy angels and the ministers of the Most High to help Her give thanks for this welcome and joyful news. The blessed Mother alternately with the seraphim and the other angels, sang the responses of a canticle that lasted for two hours. Although by their nature and supernatural gifts the angelic spirits are so subtle, wise and excellent, they were nevertheless excelled in all this by their Queen and Lady, as vassals are by their sovereign; for in Her, grace and wisdom abounded as in a Teacher, in them, only as in disciples. Having finished this canticle, humiliating Herself anew, She charged the supernatural creatures to beseech the Lord to prepare Her for her passage from mortal to eternal life, and to ask all the other angels and saints in heaven to pray for the same favour. They offered to obey Her in all things, and therewith Saint

Gabriel took leave and returned with all his company to the Empyrean heaven.

"... After placing the most blessed Mary on this exalted and supereminent throne, the Lord declared to the courtiers of heaven all the privileges She should enjoy in virtue of this participation in his majesty. The Person of the eternal Father, as the First principle of all things, speaking to the angels and saints, said to them: 'Our Daughter Mary, was chosen according to our pleasure from amongst all creatures, the first one to delight us, and who never fell from the title and position of true Daughter, such as We had given Her in our divine mind; She has a claim on our dominion, which we shall recognize by crowning Her as the legitimate and peerless Lady and Soverign'. The incarnate Word said: 'To my true and natural Mother belong all the creatures which created and redeemed by Me and of all things over which I am King. She too shall be the legitimate and supreme Queen.' The Holy Ghost said: 'Since She is called my beloved and chosen Spouse, She deserves to be crowned as Queen for all eternity.'

"Having thus spoken, the three divine Persons placed upon the head of the most blessed Mary, a crown of such new splendour and value, the like has been seen neither before nor after by any mere creature. At the same time a voice sounded from the throne saying: 'My Beloved, chosen among the creatures, our kingdom is Thine; Thou shalt be the Lady and the Soverign of the seraphim, of all the ministering spirits, the angels and of the entire universe of creatures...' Altogether festive was this day and it produced new accidental glory in the heavens. Those that partook more especially therein were her most fortunate spouse Saint Joseph, Saint Joachim and Anne and all the other relatives of the Queen, together with the thousand angels of Her Guard..."

Let us conclude this tribute to our Blessed Mother, with the words of our dear Padre Pio when, speaking on Our Lady, he said: "May Mary fill your heart with the flowers and fragrance of ever fresh virtues, and place Her maternal hand on your head. Always keep close to our Heavenly Mother, because She is the sea that must be crossed, in order to reach the shores of eternal splendour in the kingdom of Dawn."

IN PRAISE OF BLESSED MARIA

Gentle Maria - in silence, serene,
        Heaven's Queen.
In radiance, bright,
        Heavenly Light.
Crowned with stars - most fair.
        Beyond compare.
Above all others -
        Loving Mother;
Our Lord Christ is with Thee;
        Blessed Maria, pray for me.

Lorna H. Nevitt

MIRRORS OF HIS PERFECTION

As we have read throughout this book, the part of the Angels in Christian life has it's origin in the relationship they have with God and with Jesus Christ. They show us God's greatness and perfection, symbolizing individually some attributes of this Infinite Being. In some, we see His power, in others, His love or His strength. Each one of them is a reproduction of God's beauty; reflects all His perfection. Their relationship with Jesus is that of being united with Him in heaven, in order to adore, praise and glorify the heavenly Father. Hence, when we unite ourselves to

Jesus, we join, at the same time, with the Angels to adore praise and love God; thus we share with them in the Divine life. They long for our salvation so that we way join with them in the Beatific Vision.

In the history of the Church, devotion to the Guardian Angels goes way back in the centuries, but a special day of devotion was assigned to them on the 29 September; feast of Saint Michael the Archangel. In 1411, in Valencia, Spain, a special Divine Office was prepared, and in the following century, the devotion to the Guardian Angels spread out through Portugal where a franciscan priest, Giovanni Colombi, prepared another more detailed Divine Office, which was approved by Pope Leo X, in 1518. When, later on, this veneration spread throughout the Austrian Empire, Pope Clement X, established in 1670, a special feast day on 2 October.

This pious devotion to the Guardian Angels is older than that of the Saints, but in the Middle Ages, it took on an extraordinary importance because the Monks, in their silent and recollected lives, deprived of any company, searched for the companionship of these invisible creatures, so that their presence would bring joy and happiness.

In today's life, we have neglected the company of these angelic creatures; we don't feel their presence anymore. Even though they are the constant companions of our journeys and the mute witnesses of our everyday lives. It is a Church Dogma, that everyone of us, at the time of Baptism, receives an Angel, who accompanies, inspires and guides throughout the entire span of one's life. The presence of the Guardian Angels at our sides, is an invisible one; they are faithful, mute but eloquent; they are friends who remind us of our Christian duties towards God and towards our neighbours; they are the mirrors in which everyone of us has to reflect his daily behaviour.

Holy Mother Church, has developed their veneration and has taught us to live with dignity in their presence; She has taught us to turn to our Guardian Angels in the sad hours of our lives and to abandon ourselves in their arms and bestow on them, all our love, affection and confidence. Following the encouragement of the Church, let us determine, as Padre Pio did in his lifetime, to communicate more with our Guardian Angels and to unite ourselves with these celestial messengers so that, through their help, we can give praise to God and bring more souls closer to Christ. Let us listen to their beautiful words, accept their holy thoughts and follow their counsel in order that we may do good. We should never forget to thank them as they lead us along the difficult path of this life to the glory of eternal happiness.

TO THE READER

If this little book
has given you
"Food for Thought"
Then the object of
my labour
Has not been in vain
I hope also we have
been able to share
Some of Life's experiences,
And to show that we care
about the other person;
Through the medium
of the written word.
M.T.

Here, evidence of the devil's interference can be clearly seen. When Padre Pio opened this letter, it was totally illegible because of a large ink-blot covering it. However, his Guardian Angel told him to sprinkle it with holy water and, by doing this, it became legible. (see page 37).

Foggia et je [illegible] d'obtenir pour toi
les 20 messes.
Prie le bon Jésus spécialement selon
mon intention.
Réjouis dans le Seigneur: je te le souhaite
toujours. Salue de ma part les tiens, l'Ar.,
baise le petit François.
Je me dit toujours
Ton frère en J. C.

Letter dated 6 November 1912, which was written by Padre Agostino to Padre Pio. The entire letter was written in French. Padre Pio had no difficulty in understanding it's contents as his Guardian Angel translated it for him.

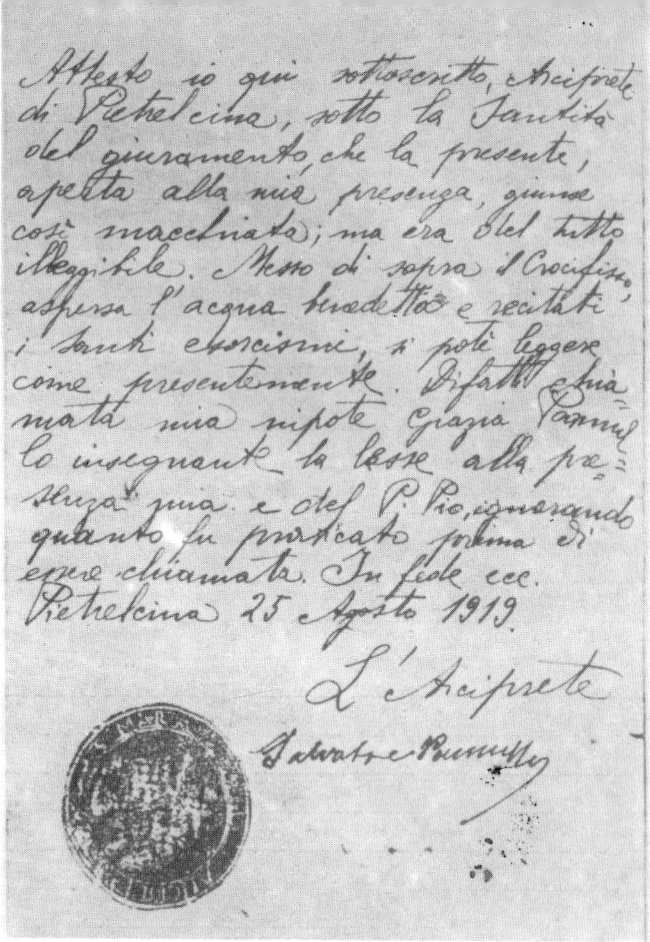
Attesto io qui sottoscritto, Arciprete
di Pietrelcina, sotto la Santità
del giuramento, che la presente,
aperta alla mia presenza, giunse
così macchiata; ma era del tutto
illeggibile. Messo di sopra il Crocifisso,
aspersa l'acqua benedetta e recitati
i santi esorcismi, si poté leggere
come presentemente. Difatti chia-
mata mia nipote Grazia Pannul-
lo insegnante la lesse alla pre-
senza mia e del P. Pio, ignorando
quanto fu praticato prima di
essere chiamata. In fede ecc.
Pietrelcina 25 Agosto 1919.

L'Arciprete

Salvatore Pannullo

This is the statement with which the Parish Priest Salvatore Pannullo certifies that the letter arrived covered with ink-blot and that it was legible only after it was sprinkled with holy water. (see page 32).

BIBLIOGRAPHY

Agostino da San Marco in Lamis, "Diario". Edited under the care of Fr. Gerardo Di Flumeri (San Giovanni Rotondo 1975, second Edition).

Alessandro da Ripabottoni, "Padre Pio da Pietrelcina. Un cireneo per tutti". Edizioni Centro Culturale Francescano, del Convento "Immacolata" (Foggia 1974).

Centro Regionale Gruppi di Preghiera di Padre Pio, "Il Sorriso di Padre Pio" (Pescara, no date given).

Costantino Capobianco, "Detti e Aneddoti di Padre Pio" Series Testimonianze 4. Edited under the care of Fr. Gerardo Di Flumeri (San Giovanni Rotondo 1973).

Curci Giuseppe, "Padre Pio e Gli Angeli" (Napoli 1973).

Edizioni L'Arcangelo, "Padre Pio Ai Suoi Figli" (San Giovanni Rotondo, undated).

Eusebio da Castelpetroso, "The Voice of Padre Pio" bi-monthly magazine of the Postulation for Padre Pio's cause. Edited by Fr. Alessio Parente, Vol. II No. 1, 1972 (San Giovanni Rotondo).

Maria of Agreda, "City of God" Series (The Coronation) Ave Maria Institute Washington (New Jersey 1971).

Massa Bonaventura, "Maria Pyle" Alla Scuola di Padre Pio (San Giovanni Rotondo 1980).

Miller C. Leslie, "All About Angels" Published by Regal Books Division (California 1973).

Mischitelli Silvestro, "Un Uomo Fuori Serie" (Foggia 1973).

McGregor Augustine, "Padre Pio - His Early Years" Edited by Fr. Alessio Parente (San Giovanni Rotondo 1981).
Morcaldi Francesco, "San Giovanni Rotondo Nella Luce Del Francescanesimo" (Rome 1950).
Paolino da Casacalenda, "Le Mie Memorie Intorno A Padre Pio" Edited under the care of Fr. Gerardo Di Flumeri (San Giovanni Rotondo 1978).
Pio da Pietrelcina, "Letters I". English version edited by Fr. Gerardo Di Flumeri (San Giovanni Rotondo 1980).
Pio da Pietrelcina, "Epistolario II". Edited under the care of Melchiorre da Pobladura and Alessandro da Ripabottoni (San Giovanni Rotondo 1975).
Pio da Pietrelcina, "Epistolario III" Edited under the care of Melchiorre da Pobladura and Alessandro da Ripabottoni (San Giovanni Rotondo 1980).
Ricci D. Nicola, "Le Grandezze Di San Michele Arcangelo" (San Giovanni Rotondo 1978).
Spaccucci Felice, "L'Ecce Homo Del Gargano" (Napoli 1971).
Schug Fr. John, "Padre Pio" Our Sunday Visitor Inc. (Indiana 1976).
Vincenzo da Casacalenda, "Padre Pio Da Pietrelcina" Testimonianze. Edited by Vincenzo da Casacalenda (San Giovanni Rotondo 1969).
The Holy Bible, Revised Standard Version Catholic Edition. London Catholic Truth Society (London 1966).

Printed by
LEONE Editrice Foggia (Italy)
March 1990